WILD HARES AND HUMMINGBIRDS

Stephen Moss is a naturalist, author, broadcaster and television producer. In a distinguished career at the BBC Natural History Unit his credits have included *Springwatch*, *Birds Britannia* and *The Nature of Britain*. He writes a monthly column on birdwatching for the *Guardian* and regularly appears on BBC Radio 4. His previous books include *The Bumper Book of Nature*, *A Bird in the Bush* and *A Sky Full of Starlings*. Originally from London, he has travelled to all seven of the world's continents in search of wildlife. He now lives with his wife and children on the Somerset Levels.

STEPHEN MOSS

Wild Hares and Hummingbirds

The Natural History of an English Village

WITH ILLUSTRATIONS BY
Harry Brockway

VINTAGE BOOKS
London

Published by Vintage 2012

2 4 6 8 10 9 7 5 3 1

First published in Great Britain in 2011 by
Square Peg

Vintage
Random House, 20 Vauxhall Bridge Road,
London SW1V 2SA

www.vintage-books.co.uk

Addresses for companies within The Random House Group Limited
can be found at: www.randomhouse.co.uk/offices.htm

The Random House Group Limited Reg. No. 954009

A CIP catalogue record for this book
is available from the British Library

ISBN 9780099552468

The Random House Group Limited supports The Forest Stewardship
Council (FSC®), the leading international forest certification
organisation. Our books carrying the FSC label are printed on FSC®
certified paper. FSC is the only forest certification scheme endorsed
by the leading environmental organisations, including Greenpeace.
Our paper procurement policy can be found at:
www.randomhouse.co.uk/environment

Type design by Chris Wakeling

Printed and bound by CPI Group (UK) Ltd, Croydon, CR0 4YY

To Brett Westwood
a fine naturalist, colleague and friend

Contents

Introduction

O F ALL THE creatures I have seen in my home village, the two most magical are wild hares and hummingbirds. Their lives rarely intersect with mine, so the times when they do are precious and memorable.

A glimpse of a long-legged animal disappearing into the night – a typical view of a hare – is something very special. No wonder our ancestors believed this leggy beast had magical powers.

A brief encounter with a hummingbird hawkmoth, as it hovers to feed on the buddleia bush in my garden, is even more exciting. Of course this aerobatic insect, a wanderer from the south, is not really a hummingbird at all. But it is still an extraordinary creature, whose mid-air manoeuvres match, and perhaps even surpass, those of its avian namesake.

These striking works of nature, the hare and the hawk-moth, are just two of the hundreds of different species – from swallows to snowdrops and badgers to bumblebees – that I come across in a typical year on my home patch.

❀

THIS QUIET, COUNTRY parish lies on the edge of the West Country, roughly halfway between the Mendip and

Polden Hills, on the misty, marshy land known as the Somerset Levels. The village at its centre is, according to local legend, the longest in England, though rivals elsewhere in the country have been known to challenge this claim.

On a clear day, if you climb the ninety-four stone steps to the top of the church tower, you can see Cheddar Gorge to the north and Glastonbury Tor to the south. The cathedral city of Wells is just out of sight to the east; while towards the west, beyond the M5 motorway, lies Bridgwater Bay, with the Quantock Hills and Exmoor beyond.

The landscape here is steeped in history: of both the natural and human kind. This is where King Arthur is said to be buried, King Alfred burned the cakes, and the last pitched battle was fought on English soil, at Sedgemoor on 6 July 1685. This is a place of wide, open skies, warm summers and chilly winters, and, above all, water. The land may appear solid and permanent, but it has been reclaimed, more recently than you might imagine, from the sea.

As in most villages up and down the country, foxes chase rabbits, badgers grub up worms, and jackdaws potter noisily around the ancient churchyard. At the height of summer, the back lanes are lined with cow parsley and willowherb, and the meadows brighten with carpets of buttercups. In winter, snowdrops force their way through the hard earth to bloom, and the calls of lapwings echo over the pale, frosty fields. From spring to autumn, the skies ring with the twittering of swallows, welcome visitors from their ancestral home in Africa.

This is more or less the sort of wildlife you would expect in any rural parish. But there are more unusual creatures here too. The small fields, with their watery boundaries, create a unique environment, full of nooks and crannies where plants and animals can thrive. So reed warblers sing their rhythmic, scratchy song from the ditches, while exquisite small copper butterflies flutter along the nearby droves. Roe deer are also found here, though they often go unnoticed because of their retiring habits. And, at dusk, a barn owl floats over waterlogged fields, on soft, silent wings.

❀

AS WELL AS the imposing sixteenth-century church, the village boasts two pubs, a post office, a village hall, a boarding school for dyslexic children, a cricket ground, a bowling green, a thriving youth theatre and a martial arts club. Well over a thousand people make their home here, many of them incomers; some from elsewhere in Somerset, others, like me and my family, from further afield.

Each year, in the middle of August, the village gathers to celebrate the traditional Harvest Home, tucking into cold meats, salads and cider, followed by games, a children's tea party, and an evening concert – the nearest we ever get to the world of rock and roll. But the most important moment of the day takes place when the guest speaker proposes a toast, and the villagers stand as one to raise their glasses 'to agriculture'.

The fields of this parish have always been productive, turning grass, fertiliser and sheer hard work into lamb, beef and strong, cloudy cider. And although nowadays far fewer people make a living from farming than in the past, the way the land is managed still has a profound influence on its natural history.

Another way we use the land, which also shapes the fortunes of the parish wildlife, is easy to overlook: the village gardens. These range from lawns the size of a pocket handkerchief, and mown to the consistency of a billiard table, to tracts of land more than an acre in size, whose owners' benign neglect has turned them into a welcome refuge for wild creatures.

As with every other community in Britain – whether in the countryside, the suburbs or the inner city – our human influence is everywhere. So if wildlife here is to survive, and especially if it is to thrive, it must live cheek by jowl with people, in our houses, barns, gardens and fields.

In recent years, like everywhere else in this crowded little island, we have witnessed great changes to our natural heritage. Older villagers recall how cuckoos used to drive them mad each spring with their incessant calling; yet nowadays the sound of the cuckoo is hardly ever heard here. Other birds have seen an upturn in their numbers during the same period. Once buzzards were shot on sight;

today, on a warm summer's morning, you may see half a dozen of these broad-winged raptors floating together in the sky. Both the decline of the cuckoo and the rise of the buzzard mirror these birds' fortunes on a national scale.

As a relative newcomer to the village, having moved down from London a few years ago, I must rely on local hearsay for evidence of these shifts in status. But even in my brief time here I have noticed changes. It was over a year before I saw my first raven, calling one autumn morning from the cider orchard alongside my home. Yet now I regularly hear the raven's deep, harsh croak, as these huge, raggedy-winged birds soar high above the village, into the blue.

❦

IT WAS GILBERT WHITE, author of *The Natural History of Selborne* (1789), who first showed us that by closely studying the wildlife of a single country parish, it was possible to draw conclusions about our wider relationship with the natural world. Now, more than two centuries later, I am following in his footsteps. By looking in depth at what happens here, in one of more than 10,000 parishes in England alone, I hope to reveal a broader truth about the current fortunes of our countryside, its people and its wildlife.

I stay mostly within the parish boundaries, an area I can comfortably explore on foot, or by bicycle, from my home. I do occasionally venture out into the surrounding area, known (to the local tourist board at least) as the Avalon Marshes, which encompasses some of the finest wild countryside in the whole of Britain.

I don't rely just on my own observations, but also enlist the help of expert naturalists, and hear from people who have lived in the village all their lives. During the course of the year I track the rhythms of the natural world: the comings and goings, the changes brought about by the seasons and the weather, and how these reflect what is going on elsewhere in the country.

This is not an easy time for Britain's wildlife. Our plants and animals must compete with the many other ways we use our limited supply of land: to grow crops and raise livestock, to build roads and homes for a growing population, and as a place for leisure and recreation. So it is more important than ever that we recognise why we need the natural world: not just for its own sake, but also to enrich our own lives.

I may have chosen to focus on one little patch of the British countryside, in and around my home village. But ultimately this is a book about the nature of Britain as a whole: what the wildlife and the places where it lives mean to every one of us.

STEPHEN MOSS
Mark, Somerset
April 2011

JANUARY

As the old year gives way to the new, a hard frost grips the land, coating every surface with a thin layer of white. The rhynes – water-filled ditches that criss-cross this flat, wintry landscape – have frozen solid. But the broader, deeper channel opposite the White Horse Inn still contains a few patches of water and mud. A couple of moorhens are feeding, their long, green toes allowing them to walk across the broken shards of ice.

Nearby, a small, hunched, brown bird with an impossibly long bill is also looking for food, optimistically probing the half-frozen mud. It is a snipe: not a local bird like the moorhens, but an immigrant from northern Europe. Earlier this winter it flew across the North Sea from Scandinavia, in search of a milder climate. It must be wondering why it bothered.

A local cyclist pedals by. The snipe stops feeding, cocks its head to one side, and crouches back on its short legs. At the last possible moment the bird springs up into the air on powerful, pointed wings – its fast, zigzagging flight designed to confuse a chasing predator, or foil a hunter with a shotgun.

As it departs, the snipe utters a curious call, rather like the sound of a muffled sneeze, or perhaps a boot being pulled out of sticky mud – an appropriate image given the bird's usual habitat. The moorhens, long used to the steady traffic of people along the edge of the rhyne, ignore the interruption and continue to feed.

❀

AT THIS TIME of year, in the dead of winter, the wildlife of the parish is best defined by what is *not* here, rather than what is – not by presence, but by absence. Four months have passed since the swallows last twittered over the barns at Mill Batch Farm; even longer since the meadows along Vole Road hummed with the sound of bumblebees, and meadowsweet and willowherb blossomed along the narrow lanes towards Chapel Allerton.

This seasonal rhythm is the key to life here, as it is all across the temperate regions of the northern hemisphere, from County Kerry in the west to Kamchatka in the east. Those swallows, bumblebees and wild flowers are not simply memories of the year now passed, but a distant promise of the spring and summer yet to come.

It is hard to believe, as I gaze over this monochrome landscape of frost, water and mud, that in just three months' time the parish will be transformed into a scene of full, glorious colour. There will be myriads of birds and flowers, insects and mammals, all engaged in the frantic race to reproduce which defines spring. This scenario will be replicated, in different ways, across this little cluster of islands, lying just off the edge of the world's greatest land mass.

4

But however hard I look now, in the dead of winter, I cannot see most of the plants and animals that make their home here in the village. Some, like the swallows and red admirals, have disappeared altogether, and are now many thousands of miles away. The swallows have travelled the farthest, all the way to the southern tip of Africa. As I and my fellow villagers shiver in the winter cold, they are swooping around the legs of elephants and giraffes, at a muddy waterhole alongside Kipling's great grey-green, greasy Limpopo River. They will remain there until the time of the spring equinox, when they will begin their long journey northwards, back to our shores.

The red admirals – those visions of elegance in black, white and orange – have not travelled quite so far. They left us back in the autumn, and flew south to the shores of the Mediterranean. There in Andalucía, home of sherry, bullfighting and flamenco, they laid their eggs; then, their mission complete, they died. Now, in the midst of our winter, their caterpillars have already emerged under warm Spanish skies, and are feeding voraciously on fresh green nettles. Soon they will pupate, and eventually, in a month or two, emerge as the next generation of adult butterflies. These, in turn, will head northwards in April; and with luck, and a following wind, will be back here in the village gardens by the end of May.

But what of the badgers and beetles, slow-worms and small tortoiseshells, newts and bats? These creatures lack both the ability and instinct to make the epic global journey of the swallow or red admiral, and must stay put for the winter. Each is now well out of sight: either in full hibernation, or simply lying low until spring finally comes, and it can resume its active life.

The badgers hide away in their underground setts, occasionally emerging to grub up earthworms and beetles to keep up their energy levels. The slow-worms, frogs and newts are tucked inside log-piles, deep in hibernation, having slowed down their metabolism close to zero for the duration of the winter. And the small tortoiseshell butterflies? They have sought out nooks and crannies in woodsheds and garages, closing their wings to hide their colourful pattern, to avoid being found and eaten by a passing wood mouse. They will remain there, torpid and motionless, until a sunny day in March, when their wings will once again unfold and take to the air, delighting those of us who are searching for signs of spring.

Yet despite the temporary disappearance of these creatures, and the bleakness of the hard, frozen landscape, there are still some signs of life. Flocks of lapwings fly over the village centre, their strong, rounded wings giving them the look of butterfly swimmers as they surge through the still, cold air. And in the tall ash trees that emerge from this horizontal landscape like city skyscrapers, glossy blue-black rooks are already inspecting last year's nests. Some carry twigs in their beaks, to make repairs, ready to lay their clutch of three or four greenish-blue eggs early in the New Year – well before the leaves are on the trees.

Along the lanes leading out of the village, fieldfares and redwings throng the hedgerows, greedily gulping down the last remaining berries. These smart, colourful thrushes are winter visitors, who arrived last autumn from the north and east, in search of food. Food is also the top priority for the sparrows, robins, tits and finches congregating in the centre of the village, where my fellow parishioners generously provide kitchen scraps, nuts and seeds to keep the birds alive at this difficult time.

Whether these small birds survive the winter depends on two things: the prevailing weather pattern – either mild and damp, or cold and snowy – and the food and water we provide. Only when spring finally comes will we in the parish, and in towns and villages throughout Britain, discover the fate of these, some of our best-loved wild creatures.

❧

THE PARISH CHURCH is by far the tallest and most impressive building in the village – a landmark visible from every corner of the parish, and often beyond. It is the oldest of our man-made structures: dating back to just before the Norman Conquest, when the village itself is first mentioned in historical documents, although the building was restored and rebuilt between the late fourteenth and early sixteenth centuries. Today, the church tower sports a large clock, installed for Queen Victoria's Golden Jubilee in 1887; and a fine set of bells, which still ring for weddings and parish festivals.

Whenever the solid grey tower hoves into view, I imagine one of our ancestors using it to find his way through this flat, and often featureless, landscape. Walking the dozen miles from Brent Knoll to Glastonbury Tor, he would have passed just to the west and south of the church, before heading out across the bleak wastes of Tealham and Tadham Moors, his feet splashing through the flooded fields as he passed. Continuing through the ancient settlements of Meare and Godney, he would finally reach the safety of high ground, on the tor itself.

The church still plays an important part in the life of the village community. In the hallowed ground surrounding the building, a scattering of gravestones marks the resting places of the ancestors of many of today's villagers. The names carved here – many so weathered as to be almost illegible – are a tribute to the longevity of the main local families. There are Puddys and Pophams, Ducketts and Fears – with no fewer than ten members of the latter family buried beneath a single, imposing headstone.

As well as what it tells us about the human history of the parish, the churchyard also has a crucial role to play in its natural history. In the British countryside, where almost every scrap of land has been ploughed, planted with crops, or sprayed with pesticides, churchyards are among the few places that remain largely untouched by progress.

In a world of rapid and unpredictable change, the

churchyard has become a precious haven for plants and animals. The notion of 'sanctuary' may have lost much of its original meaning, but for the wildlife of a country parish like this, churchyards do offer a refuge hard to find elsewhere.

In the middle of January, though, the casual observer may be forgiven for wondering where all this natural life has gone. But frost is not the only thing covering the graves. For here, surrounded by eternal reminders of death, is a particularly tenacious form of life: lichens. In this churchyard, as in churchyards all over Britain, they are everywhere: on the surface of the gravestones, covering the trunks and branches of the trees, and smothering the walls of the building itself, especially on the damp, shady side.

Although we often think of lichens as lower forms of plant life, they are the outward form of a complex symbiotic relationship between a fungus and an alga. They may have humble origins, but are nevertheless extraordinarily successful. Paradoxically, it is their very ubiquity which renders lichens invisible to the casual viewer. They are an integral part of the living landscape, almost seeming to infect the brick, wood and stone surfaces they grow on. But when I pull off my glove and run my hand across the cold surface of an ancient gravestone, the lichens flake off, leaving a greenish-grey stain on my palm.

Like these gravestones, and the church itself, lichens go way back in time. Some of those here today may have already been in existence when the newly crowned King James II defeated his rival the Duke of Monmouth, down the road at Sedgemoor, in 1685. Others could be even older: for one lichen-covered stone, now weathered beyond readability, predates the current sixteenth-century building. The surface of this huge, flat slab is home to dozens of different lichen colonies of varying hues, from mustard-yellow, through moss-green, to a clean, icy grey. Together they create that pleasingly soft-edged effect familiar to all country churchyards.

What a contrast with the polished, black marble headstones in the new cemetery just along the road, where the village's more recently departed souls lie in rest.

❀

ANOTHER ANCIENT FEATURE of the parish churchyard is equally easy to overlook. As I walk around the gravestones, I pass beneath compact, bushy trees with dense, bottle-green foliage. Come the autumn, these will be dotted with bright, plastic-looking, orange-red berries, much beloved of the local thrushes and blackbirds.

These are yews; along with juniper and Scots pine, one of only three conifer species native to Britain. Yews are also our most ancient living thing, with some specimens, such as the Fortingall Yew in a Perthshire churchyard, well over two thousand years old. And of all Britain's native trees, the yew is the one most closely associated with churchyards.

The reasons for this connection are buried deep in

our distant past. The yew's legendary longevity meant that it was often planted by our pre-Christian ancestors, as a symbol of long life. Many parish churches – probably including this one – were built on existing pagan sites. We know from the eighteenth-century historian John Collinson that 'a fine old yew tree in a decaying state' was still growing here in 1791, and would have dated back much earlier.

There is another reason why yews are often found in churchyards. Their leaves, bark and seeds are poisonous to livestock (and indeed to humans), so they may have been deliberately planted to discourage farmers from letting their animals graze in the church grounds. The yew also owes its survival to the flexible qualities of its wood, which made it especially suitable for making the weapon of choice in early medieval England: the longbow.

❈

AS I WALK past the churchyard, I hear a distinctive sound coming from the dense, dark foliage of the yew trees. A high-pitched, rhythmic snatch of birdsong, almost childlike in its tone and pattern – 'diddly-diddly-diddly-diddly-deeee'. This is the sound of the smallest bird in the parish, and indeed the smallest in Britain: the goldcrest. Tiny, plump, and decked in pastel shades of green, the goldcrest can sometimes be glimpsed as it flits around the outer foliage of the yews, before plunging back into the dark interior.

This creature is a true featherweight, tipping the scales

at just one-fifth of on ounce: about the same as a twenty-pence coin, or a single sheet of A4 paper. Small size is bad news if you want to survive during long spells of cold weather. The smaller you are, the higher your ratio of surface area to volume; which means that a bird the size of a goldcrest loses heat very rapidly indeed. So like other small birds, it must feed constantly through the short winter days, to get enough energy to keep it alive through the long, cold nights.

Most insect-eating birds don't even try to survive the British winter; instead they head south to warmer climes, where food is easier to find. But the goldcrest has a secret weapon: its association with evergreens such as the yew. Because these trees don't shed their leaves in winter, their dense foliage is home to thousands of tiny insects. The goldcrest is the only bird small enough to survive on these minuscule creatures, and will spend the coldest months of the year inside our churchyard yews; feeding by day, and huddled up for warmth by night.

On bright, sunny days, even in the middle of winter, I occasionally see the male goldcrest puffing up his chest, momentarily flashing his golden crown like a shaft of sunlight piercing through a winter sky, and issuing a burst of song. It is a curiously optimistic sound for this time of year, and a reminder that however cold the weather may still be, spring will eventually arrive.

❀

BUT NOT QUITE yet. Overnight, an unexpected, silent visitor has come to the village. Powering southwards down the length of England, across the Cotswold and Mendip Hills, it reached here in the early hours. As dawn breaks, we open our curtains to a landscape transformed into a sea of white. Our village, the county and the whole country have come to a standstill, in the worst winter weather for thirty years.

The village children can hardly believe their luck. A cheery local radio announcer confirms what they all hope to hear: school has been cancelled. And every child, in every home, has undergone a miraculous transformation. Clothes have been pulled on, breakfasts eaten up, and coats, boots and gloves donned with joyful enthusiasm. They can hardly wait to get out of the door – not for their lessons, but to play with an unfamiliar and exciting substance: snow.

With the snow still falling, all is silent. Apart from the occasional sparrow's chirp from the hedgerow along the lane, I hear nothing. The birds are far too busy to think of anything other than finding something to eat. If they fail to do so, they will die – and soon. Cold weather on its own will not kill birds, but snow does: for it covers up their food supplies. So the arrival of this white blanket from the north is very bad news indeed.

Which is why, since first light, the bird-feeders outside my kitchen window have been chock-full of birds. As well as the usual great tits and goldfinches there are greenfinches, chaffinches – even a pied wagtail, grimly clinging on to the feeder as he pecks at the life-giving seeds within.

The snow acts like a photographer's reflector, making the birds glow with unexpected clarity. Familiar species appear, quite literally, in a new light: the olive-green of the greenfinch, orange-red of the robin, and brick-coloured breast of the chaffinch all enhanced by this natural uplighter.

Livestock means warmth, and in Mill Batch farmyard a morose-looking herd of dairy cows has attracted a flock of starlings. Some birds are perched on the telegraph wires above, but most are sitting on the backs of the cattle, enjoying the benefit of warmth from the weighty bodies of these huge beasts, as they munch on a fresh supply of hay. For one brief moment the starlings remind me of oxpeckers perched on big game, in the heat-haze of the African savannah.

Out in the fields, where the wind blows the falling snow almost horizontally across the flat land, nothing stirs. All wild creatures have sought shelter. Even the sheep have forsaken their usual feeding places, and are huddled together in a corner of the apple orchard; where the dirty yellow of their wool presents a stark contrast with the all-new whiteness of their surroundings.

❀

FOR THE BUZZARD perched on top of an ash tree by Perry Farm, peering down upon a landscape of white and grey, life goes on, though rather more slowly than usual. Buzzards, like all large birds of prey, take a lot of effort to get airborne; so during the winter they conserve their energy by staying put for most of the day.

As I approach, his piercing yellow eyes stare intently at this intruder into his space. He lifts his tail, and empties his bowels in preparation for flight. A moment later, he spreads his broad wings and launches himself into the air, every flap a major effort. He is joined by his mate, and they gradually gain height in the chilly air, attracting the attention of a lone crow feeding in the nearby field. The crow may be about half the weight of a buzzard, but he is still prepared to have a go at his larger rivals. As often happens, the smaller bird wins the skirmish, and the buzzards head off.

I move on too, down the icy lane, enjoying the clear blue sky and windless conditions. A farmer has put out a bale of straw for his sheep, and they line up patiently to feed, shuffling slowly forward like pensioners waiting to board a bus. Turning westwards, I head along the broad, straight track between Binham Moor and Kingsway. Like many of the paths criss-crossing this and other local parishes, this is a 'drove' – a vital means of moving livestock from one place to another, across this watery landscape.

The first droves were made in Anglo-Saxon times, but their heyday was during the late Middle Ages, when a rapidly growing urban population needed food from the surrounding countryside. Sheep, pigs, cattle and geese would all have been driven down these tracks to be sold at market. Only with the coming of the railways in the nineteenth century did this custom eventually decline. But the droves themselves remain: allowing me to venture off the metalled roads and lanes, and into the heart of the countryside.

On such a calm, clear day, the sound of my feet trudging through deep snow creates a pleasingly soporific rhythm, in contrast to the silent world all around. My mind begins to wander until, along a sunlit hedgerow, a sudden burst of song jolts me out of my daydream. It comes from a tiny, chestnut-brown bird, flitting up from the base of the hedge above the frozen rhyne. It is a wren, so small it would fit into my hand, yet with a very loud voice. I wonder why it is singing on such a bitterly cold day, when in answer to my question – and the wren's – comes a second burst of song, from a rival male barely 10 yards away. I have stumbled across the boundary between two territories, where later in the spring these adversaries will – if they survive the winter – fight for the right to breed.

Along the first stretch of the drove, the snow is covered with footprints, and the outlines of horses' hooves. But after passing through a rusty gate, I find pure, fresh snow, save for the tracks of a pair of roe deer, and the prints of a fox. A disconcerting crunch beneath my feet reminds me that beneath the thick layer of snow there is a much thinner layer of ice, with water beneath. Fortunately, it is firm enough to bear my weight.

The last time I walked along this drove, during the height of summer, I was serenaded by the sound of birdsong, amid fluttering painted lady and small copper butterflies. Now, as I scan the fields on either side, my breath steaming in the icy air, I see nothing – not even the roe deer that passed this way earlier.

❀

AS THE HARDEST winter for thirty years rapidly turns into the worst in my memory, the birds are flocking to the centre of the village; into my garden, and those of my neighbours. Outside our kitchen window there is a scene of almost constant activity; even before the weak winter sun has risen, the birds are gathering, desperate to feed.

Even in this dim half-light they are easy to pick out, especially the blackbird, dark against the white ground, his short legs sinking into the snow. Once the sun is up the whole gang is here: blue tits and great tits gathering on the feeders; song thrushes and dunnocks beneath, picking up the spilt seed; and robins, vainly trying to defend their little patch of snow-covered lawn against their bitter rivals.

The robins look almost indecently fat and healthy, but this is a cruel illusion. The only way these birds will survive is if they can preserve what little warmth they still have in their bodies, so they fluff up their feathers in an attempt to do so. Many are losing the battle, and with each night that passes, a share of the birds that visited us the day before will now be dead.

My youngest son George is fascinated by all this activity, and loves to stand at the kitchen sink to watch. He is getting pretty good at naming the birds; though I am sceptical when he confidently announces the presence of a redwing. But it turns out he is right – this small, dark, northern thrush is indeed here in our garden. And we're not alone. Reports from all over the country confirm that redwings, along with their larger cousins the fieldfares, are heading into our gardens to search for food.

About a million individuals of each species arrived in the country back in October and November, with a good number reaching this parish. During the autumn and early winter they flock along the hawthorn hedgerows, grabbing as many berries as they can. By January they have usually switched to feeding in muddy fields, where they forage for worms in the loamy soil. But with snow now covering the earth, and most berries having been eaten, they have no choice but to join their more familiar relatives in our gardens.

The huge difference between this and past 'big freezes' is that these birds will find plenty of good-quality, high-energy food; provided, of course, by us. Even in the last freeze-up, back in 1979, bird-feeding was not particularly widespread; and in 1963, 1947 and 1940 – the twentieth century's other long, hard winters – it was in comparison almost non-existent.

Many of the older villagers can still recall the winter of 1947 – the second coldest in living memory. This was before the days of central heating, while post-war rationing meant there was little or no food to spare for the birds. What a contrast with today, when millions of us up and down the country provide not just kitchen scraps but designer foodstuffs for our garden birds. I reflect that we – and the birds – have never had it so good.

❀

BUT I ONLY need to walk down the lane that runs behind our house, towards the little hamlet of Perry, to realise that for birds which cannot seek refuge in the village gardens life is still very tough. I see signs of desperation everywhere I look. A gaggle of moorhens pick their way across a small patch of snow, marginally less deep than the rest of the field. The rhyne below, where they would normally find their food, is frozen solid.

Further along, a small, slender bird is fluttering weakly across the ice: hunched, grey, with a sliver of lemon-yellow peeking out from beneath its long tail. It is a grey wagtail, hardly recognisable as the graceful creature I am used to seeing. Feeding mainly on tiny insects, often picked from the surface of the water, the grey wagtail is perhaps the most vulnerable bird in the parish to ice and snow. I don't imagine this bird will survive more than another night or two.

Even large waterbirds face the same fate. On the marshes a few miles south of here, bitterns and water rails are forsaking their reclusive habits and coming out into the open, desperate to find something – anything – to eat. As I drive the children back from school, along the ice rink that used to be the road, we pass a hunched, forlorn creature, perched pathetically on a wooden gate: the local heron. He looks as if he has given up all hope, and with all the surrounding waterways covered with ice, perhaps he is right.

Not every creature suffers from the harsh weather. The buzzards sit and wait, occasionally flapping across the countryside in search of something dead or dying. Foxes, too, are out in force. There are plenty of opportunities for both predators and scavengers here in this frozen landscape.

And once the snow and ice have finally melted, what are the prospects for Britain's birds? Come the spring, it is likely that vulnerable species such as the wren, long-tailed tit, goldcrest, kingfisher and grey heron will be here in much lower numbers than usual.

But if we take the longer view, we realise that this winter is part of a pattern of extreme weather events, a pattern these birds have evolved to cope with. Small birds only live a year or two, producing large broods of young to compensate for their brief lifespan. So in three or four years' time, when this winter is but a distant memory, their numbers will probably be more or less back to normal.

There may even be benefits from a return to what the newspapers are calling a 'proper' winter. Diseases and parasites are killed off by a long cold spell; while hibernating creatures such as hedgehogs will stay fast asleep, rather than emerging too early as they do in mild winters. And this spring is likely to be 'on time' compared with recent years, when unseasonably warm weather has encouraged birds to lay their eggs as early as January, only to be hit by freezing weather in February or March, which cuts off their food supply and kills their chicks.

❁

EVENTUALLY, OF COURSE, the cold spell does come to an end, and the snow retreats as rapidly as it arrived. The first weekend after the thaw, the landscape is back to its normal winter state: soggy mush. The rhynes are full to the brim, the layer of ice now replaced with a thin film of duckweed, punctured only by the occasional discarded drinks can.

The birds are back, too. A song thrush, the first I have heard this year, sings his famously repetitive tune in the tall trees by the village stores. Blackbirds feed beneath the hedgerows, while jackdaws, rooks and crows grub up worms in the muddy fields, just as they did before the snow came.

As I cycle along River Road, towards the southern boundary of the parish, I hear a familiar high-pitched note. There is a movement in the corner of my vision, and I spy a grey wagtail as it flies away, the telltale lemon patch beneath its tail reflecting the morning sun. Despite my fears this individual, at least, has managed to survive.

I hide my bicycle behind a convenient hedge, and walk across a muddy field; deeply rutted with tractor tracks, and dotted with patches of standing water. A familiar sound – perhaps *the* sound of the countryside – comes from somewhere ahead of me, but with the sun shining straight into my eyes I cannot see the bird that is making it. I skirt around to get a better view, past a clump of mole-hills, and realise, to my surprise, that there are more than a hundred birds feeding here. Most are redwings, with their usual companions, a dozen or so fieldfares; and a couple of meadow pipits.

Then I see what I am looking for, a short way from the main flock: three sandy-coloured birds, their paleness standing out against the dark, loamy soil. They are skylarks, the iconic British farmland bird; yet here in the parish, hardly a common sight. This is partly because the ground is almost permanently soggy, unsuitable for arable crops. But it is also because like so many of our familiar countryside birds, the skylark has suffered a catastrophic decline, numbers falling by more than half in my own lifetime.

When amateur birders all over Britain took part in the British Trust for Ornithology's first *Atlas* survey, back in the late 1960s, the skylark was Britain's most widespread bird. Today, both its population and range have contracted dramatically. Modern farming methods – industrial processes that have no place for, or concern with, nature – are largely responsible. But those of us who enjoy cheap food, and the convenience of supermarkets, must also bear our share of the blame. For if we cannot safeguard a bird as intrinsic to our landscape as the skylark, what hope is there for rest of the countryside and its wildlife?

On sunny days in early spring, I do occasionally hear the song of the skylark, as it flies high in the skies above the parish fields. Straining my eyes to find this almost invisible dot, I marvel at its ability to sing constantly for hours on end. But my pleasure is tinged by sadness, as I think about the two million or more pairs of skylarks we have lost in the short time that I have been on this earth.

❀

BY THE END of the month, the snow is but a distant memory, though patches of ice still persist in the shadier corners of the parish. On fine, sunny days the sky now glows blue with the distant promise of spring. Just above the Mendips, there is a long, thin layer of smoky cloud, as a lone hot-air balloon drifts upwards, and an easyJet plane descends slowly towards Bristol airport.

Just like the snow, the mud along the droves reveals

what has passed by: the paw-prints and horseshoes of the local hunt, whose hounds, horses and green-clad riders entertained the village children as they came past earlier in the day, in pursuit of a local fox.

Until I came to Somerset, my experience of foxes was confined to those I saw in Bristol or London. There, if I came across a fox it would stand its ground, facing me defiantly until I gave in and walked away. How very different from Somerset foxes, which have developed the art of self-preservation not needed by their city cousins.

When I wander down to the end of my garden and find a fox asleep in a sheltered, sunny corner, the sheer sense of panic as it wakes is extraordinary. Even during the heavy snow, when I watched a large dog fox padding purposefully across a field, I knew that when he caught sight of me he would head off in the opposite direction – which is exactly what he did.

The thaw has revealed signs of another, even more elusive mammal, the mole, with masses of molehills appearing at the edges of grassy fields. I recall my grandmother telling me that her father – my great-grandfather – was the proud owner of a genuine moleskin waistcoat; which he presumably obtained from the local mole-catcher. But nobody bothers to trap moles any more – they either put up with the damage to their fields and lawns, or call in the pest controllers to poison them.

As we wait for February to arrive, the lengthening days and imperceptible rising of the sun in the sky signal that spring is, if not quite around the corner, nevertheless on its way. The birds sense this too: increased day length triggers sensors in their tiny brains, prompting them to embark on one of the most wasteful and dangerous, yet most vital and beautiful, aspects of their behaviour: birdsong.

Wasteful because they can ill-afford to expend so much energy; dangerous because singing draws attention to their presence, making them vulnerable to predators. Yet vital, because if a male bird does not sing, he will be unable to defend his territory and win a mate; and if he cannot do that, he will not be able to breed this year. If he fails to breed, he may never get a second chance.

And beautiful? Yes: because even though we now understand the scientific reasons for this behaviour, we cannot help but be overwhelmed by its sheer beauty.

January sees the early starters in the breeding race begin to sing. In my garden, robins lead the way: sometimes uttering their sweet, deliberate and tuneful song on New Year's Day itself. During mild winters, robins are joined by a chorus of other garden birds, each determined to get a head start on their rivals. So great tits sing their brash 'tea-cher, tea-cher' from the bare branches of the apple trees, while goldfinches twitter in the hawthorn hedge.

Later in the year, as spring finally takes hold, these early birds will be joined by new arrivals: the migrants currently spending our winter thousands of miles away in Africa. And day by day, week by week and month by month, other creatures will emerge: insects and mammals, reptiles and amphibians, and the panoply of wild flowers that will grace the parish fields and byways all summer long.

It is a gradual process, an unseen hand weaving a complex tapestry of sight and sound, smell and colour, by which the nature of this parish – and of country parishes all over Britain – begins to reveal itself. As each day, week, month and season passes by, the picture finally takes shape, reaching its full glory with the approach of the summer solstice. Then, as the year begins to turn, and the days imperceptibly shorten, an equally gradual retreat will begin. Little by little, we shall witness the decline, departure and disappearance of the plants and animals that make up the natural history of our little part of the world.

Like a film being run backwards, the tapestry will start to unravel; slowly at first, then more rapidly, as we head towards autumn, then winter. Finally, at the close of the year, we return to how things were; seemingly unchanged, yet subtly different from where we began. But for now, at the end of the first month of the year, the annual cycle has yet to run its course, with all the joy, wonder and surprise this will bring.

FEBRUARY

OUR VILLAGE FIRST appears in the historical record more than a thousand years ago, in AD 973. Almost a century later Queen Edith, the wife of King Edward the Confessor, granted this little patch of land to the church at Wells. She is commemorated in the name of a hamlet just outside the parish: Edithmead.

Another local place name suggests that people may have settled here even earlier. Totney, a farm at the eastern end of the village, means 'look-out island' in Anglo-Saxon. It rests on a narrow tongue of higher ground, rising a few yards above the surrounding land, meaning that our ancestors could have kept their feet dry here. For like those other great English wetlands, the Fens and the Broads, the landscape of the Somerset Levels is both made up of and defined by water.

Today, as I gaze out from the top of the church tower, the surrounding land gives every impression of being as solid and permanent as anywhere else in lowland England. But this is an illusion, for these green fields were once beneath the waves. At the time Queen Edith made her gift, much of this 'landscape' was essentially a seascape: saltmarsh, inundated twice a day by the tides.

The story of how saltmarsh was gradually turned into brackish marsh, then freshwater grazing meadows, and finally dry land, is an extraordinary one. It involved hard work, of course, but also vision: the vision to realise that the land could, with time and effort, be reclaimed from the sea. Like all great human achievements, it also required a degree of arrogance; as one writer has noted, 'men have played God with water on the levels for more years than can be comprehended'. Or, as one local told me: 'we couldn't raise the land, so we lowered the water instead'.

In its pristine, original state, this landscape must have been a precious haven for those creatures that depended on water, such as wading birds and wildfowl. People came here too, regularly visiting the area from higher ground, to catch fish, trap waterbirds for food, and kill otters and beavers for their fur.

We know this because of a remarkable discovery made in 1970 at Westhay, a short distance to the south-east of the parish. A man digging peat unearthed the remains of an ancient pathway, made from wooden poles and planks of oak, and later named (after its discoverer) the Sweet Track. Using the method of studying tree rings known as dendrochronology, its construction was dated to the year 3806 BC, making it almost six thousand years old – the oldest properly constructed roadway found so far anywhere in the world.

Later, around two centuries before the birth of Christ, archaeological deposits reveal that the inhabitants of Iron Age Glastonbury caught, killed and ate Dalmatian pelicans, a huge, now globally threatened bird, long extinct here in Britain.

❀

THE LONG, SLOW process of reclaiming the land from the sea began in medieval times, when the monks of Glastonbury hired men to dig ditches across this bleak and treacherous land. Ditches and rhynes allowed water to drain into the three rivers that cross this part of Somerset: the Parrett, the Brue and the Axe. Later, sea walls were built to prevent storm surges and high tides from flooding the low-lying land behind the coast.

Today, a waterway still runs just west of due north past the White Horse Inn, between Vole Road and Kingsway. It is easy to miss from the road: a deep trench, 5 or 6 yards wide, edged with grass and reeds. In winter it often ices over, while during the summer it is carpeted with a thick, lime-green layer of duckweed.

This slow-moving body of water may not look very significant, yet it holds the key to the history of this parish. Without it the pubs, the shop, the church hall, the cricket ground, the homes, the gardens and the rest of village life simply wouldn't exist. For this stagnant, neglected waterway was the key weapon in the battle to win land from sea.

Records from Glastonbury Abbey dating back to the middle of the thirteenth century refer to it as the Morditch. Today, the Ordnance Survey map shows it as the Pillrow Wall Rhyne, while the locals call it Mark Yeo. Finished in 1316, early in the reign of Edward II, it ran all the way from Glastonbury, via the River Axe, to Bridgwater Bay: a distance of some fifteen miles. Tidal along the whole of its length, it allowed seagoing barges to bring goods and people across the waterlogged land, until the early sixteenth century, when Henry VIII's Dissolution of the Monasteries led to its eventual decline.

But despite the draining and reclamation of the land, the battle was far from won. On 20 January 1607, observers reported seeing what appeared to be a bank of fog drifting in from the sea. In fact it was a vast wall of water, possibly a tsunami caused by an undersea earthquake, which breached the sea walls and poured over the land beyond. By the time the waters came to a stop, at the foot of Glastonbury Tor, hundreds of square miles of Somerset had been flooded, a score of villages devastated, and more than a thousand people were dead. Rabbits were seen floating on swimming sheep, while a baby in a wooden cradle was miraculously rescued from the floodwaters.

Less than a century later, an even more devastating event occurred. On the night of 26 November 1703, the worst storm ever to hit Britain swept up the Severn Estuary, pushing vast amounts of water upriver. As the estuary narrowed into a funnel, the water could no longer be contained, and just as it had in 1607, the sea burst through the coastal defences and onto the low-lying land. Once again, hundreds of people drowned, along with thousands of sheep and cattle; incredibly, one seagoing ship was found more than fifteen miles inland.

Following these disasters sea walls were strength-ened, rivers straightened and rhynes dug, creating the landscape I see around me today. The lives of local people were transformed. Sheep could now be grazed without the constant problem of foot-rot, which had previously killed thousands of animals. The effects on the local wildlife are less easy to quantify: wetland species must inevitably have declined, while those that lived on farmland would have increased in numbers.

Yet despite all these efforts, the people who live in these low-lying lands are well aware that their homes are still vulnerable to extreme weather and high tides. Only the maintenance of sea walls, the regular pumping of rainwater off the land each winter, and constant vigilance, keep us safe from flooding. This is still, essentially, a landscape dominated by water in all its forms, eloquently described by local poet William Diaper, writing soon after the Great Storm of 1703:

> *Eternal mists their dropping curse distill*
> *And drizzly vapours all the ditches fill:*
> *The swamp land's a bog, the fields are seas*
> *And too much moisture is the grand disease.*

❀

Unlike most properties in the village our home is well removed from any risk of flooding, being at the eastern end, a short distance from the boundary with the neighbouring parish of Wedmore, and about 50 feet above sea level. In this part of Somerset this qualifies as the uplands, and the wind certainly whips across our land with more ferocity than in the lower parts of the parish. Taking advantage of this, the mill which gives our property its name, Mill Batch, was built here in the early eighteenth century, though it was dismantled long before we arrived.

Viewed from the air, our 1½-acre plot is surprisingly long and narrow, approximately 300 yards long by 30 yards wide, running northwards alongside the lane to the hamlet of Perry. The house was once the main dwelling for the farm next door, whose yard is still in regular use.

Our garden is about as wooded as you get in these parts: with cider-apple trees along the west side, a row of pollarded willows along the east, and two majestic ash trees at the far end. It slopes downwards, becoming less like a garden and more like an unkempt meadow the further you go. At the very bottom there is a boggy area, with a small patch of shaded, stagnant water surrounded by bramble bushes and nettles.

The next-door garden has more mature ash trees, in the tops of which are a rookery, whose inhabitants provide the soundtrack to our lives from March through to August. Across the lane there is a large apple orchard: a mixture of cider-apple trees with their bitter yellow fruit, and fine eaters of a wonderfully deep shade of red. Sheep often graze here, wandering among the dappled light.

Overall, as with most gardens, the mixture of 'mini-habitats' combined with a plentiful supply of food – both natural and provided by us – creates a home for an extraordinary range of plants and animals. In our time here I have recorded almost eighty different species of bird, over a hundred different moths, and a score of butterflies – more than one third of all Britain's species.

Badgers leave telltale trails across the meadow and deep holes on the lawn; foxes bask on the remains of a bonfire; voles and mice scurry through the long grass; and toads, slow-worms and grass snakes live unobtrusively in the hidden corners – occasionally revealing their presence, as when adventuring toads crawl purposefully into our hallway.

It is no coincidence that the British are a nation of wild-life watchers as well as a nation of gardeners, as the two go hand in hand. Our obsession with not only owning but planting and nurturing our little piece of land has created a haven for wildlife, and enabled us to enjoy watching it. Natural curiosity plays its part – and as a result, many of us now know the fauna and flora of our own garden by heart.

❦

EVERY YEAR, A song thrush holds territory in our front garden, starting to sing sometime between the middle of January and early February, depending on the severity of the winter. Even before I open the bedroom curtains each morning, I can hear him.

The annual switch between the opposing states of silence and song is like a light coming on. For once he starts singing, he seems unable to stop, like a cyclist careering downhill without any brakes. Every day, from dawn until dusk, he perches high in the branches of an ivy-covered ash sapling, its twigs just about to come into bud. Sitting out in the open, in full view, he simply opens his bill and lets the flow of notes and phrases emerge.

A hundred yards to the north, at the other end of the garden, another thrush answers him. From now onwards, as I cycle along the parish lanes, just as the song of one bird fades behind me so the next starts up ahead; a relay of thrushes, continuing for hundreds of miles in every direction, throughout the British countryside.

As its name suggests, the song thrush is justly famed for its musical ability. Both Thomas Hardy and Robert Browning wrote poems celebrating this: Hardy's 'Darkling Thrush' and Browning's 'Home-thoughts, from Abroad'. Of the two, I prefer Browning's, which uses the jagged metre of the verse to mimic the rhythm of the bird's song:

> *That's the wise thrush; he sings each song twice over,*
> *Lest you should think he never could recapture*
> *The first fine careless rapture!*

But Hardy's portrait is quietly evocative:

> *An aged thrush, frail, gaunt, and small,*
> *In blast-beruffled plume,*
> *Had chosen thus to fling his soul*
> *Upon the growing gloom.*

I have always had a sneaking suspicion, however, that Hardy may be referring to a mistle thrush, a songster that begins very early in the year (Hardy's poem is set at the close of December, rather than in Browning's springtime), and is well known for continuing to sing, even during strong winter winds – hence its folk name of 'stormcock'.

As I go about my daily chores I can hear the thrush's song, the sound penetrating through the thick, ancient walls to reach my ear wherever I am in the house. Its repetitive, measured rhythm makes it one of the most characteristic of all British birdsongs, and among the easiest to recognise. To me, it always seems as if the bird is addressing the listener directly – conducting a conversation, if you like. But it is a fairly one-sided conversation: the thrush hardly stops to pause for breath, let alone allow me to answer him.

I am reminded of a story my grandmother used to tell me when I was a child. She recalled her father, Edgar Snow, telling her that when he was a young man in Devonshire a bird would call out his name, coupled with a pecuniary instruction: 'Snowy, Snowy – Pay the rent! Pay the rent!' The songster could only have been a song thrush – no other common bird is quite so direct and insistent in its vocal style.

So whenever I hear 'my' song thrush, or indeed any other, my mind is taken back almost a century, to the years before the First World War, when my great-grandfather was amused by the song of one of this bird's distant ancestors.

❁

IN THE NEIGHBOURING village of Blackford, half a mile to the east, the rooks are already checking out their nests in the churchyard. Rooks love churchyards, for one simple reason. In the past, these holy places would have been one of the few places these glossy blue-black birds would have been safe from the shotgun. Loathed for their habit of flocking together to feed on grain, and for their alleged attacks on newborn lambs, rooks have always been regarded as the farmer's enemy.

In another sense, though, the farmer is the rook's friend. For before the neolithic ancestors of today's farmers first tilled the soil and grew crops, rooks must have been far less common and widespread. Today they are the quintessential bird of open fields, found throughout rural Britain. Generally ignored, by birdwatchers as well as by ordinary folk, they deserve more attention than they usually get; though I confess that I, too, often take them for granted.

Across the road from the churchyard stands the old school, founded in 1832, its function clearly declared on a plaque displayed inside the building:

> *For the purpose of educating the children of the poor in the Chapelry of Blackford, according to the principles of the Established Church.*

The school has long since been converted into the village hall, where the locals gather for children's birthday parties, ballet lessons and community events. But older villagers still recall that during particularly wet winters, some pupils used to arrive by boat; and although winter flooding is no longer as extensive as it once was, the route from the south may still sometimes be navigable.

Meanwhile, the season is advancing slowly but surely, in tiny, almost unnoticeable increments, marked by the marginally later arrival of sunset each day. So at four o'clock on a cold and windy afternoon in early February, there is just enough light for boys and girls from the local school to come and play before they catch the bus home. Full of pent-up energy, they chase each other around the playground, blissfully unaware that, close by, one of the first true signs of spring has already begun to emerge.

As I sit and watch my own children on the slide and swings, I notice something out of the corner of my eye. A lone hazel tree, in the hedgerow separating the playground from the next field, is covered with bunches of long, greenish-yellow catkins. They hang in groups of three or four, each catkin about the length of my thumb, and superficially resembling a rather thin caterpillar in shape. Like newborn lambs and Easter bunnies, hazel catkins are one of the key events of early spring – an association which, along with their drooping appearance, has given them the country name of 'lamb's tails'.

Although we call them catkins, they are in fact flowers – but flowers that don't have to wait until later in the season to bloom. Because their pollen is carried by the wind, rather than insects, it is better for the catkins to appear when there are no leaves on the trees to block the pollen's spread. Hence their emergence so early, often when there is still snow on the ground.

But these long, showy objects only tell half the story. They are all male, while the female flowers are so small and unobtrusive it is easy to miss them. I look more closely, and can just make out a tiny crimson tuft sprouting out of a swollen bud: the female flower. Once pollination has occurred, and the flower has been fertilised, it will begin to grow into a cluster of nuts. These will slowly ripen until early autumn, when they will fall to the ground below, providing much-needed food for woodpeckers, voles and wood mice.

Archaeologists have discovered that towards the end of the Middle Stone Age, about 6,000 or 7,000 years ago, the hazel spread rapidly north and west, far beyond its original home range. I imagine a hungry traveller grabbing a handful of hazelnuts to quell his appetite, picking some more to eat later, then heading off on his journey. Later on, he must have dropped or discarded them; and by this happy accident the tree spread northwards, so that today, it can be found throughout Britain.

❀

FROM THE HIGH point of the parish church, Little Moor Road winds slowly downhill towards the south-east. It runs past a modern housing estate, a field of alpacas and a sign selling horse manure, before reaching large, open fields, full of fieldfares and lapwings.

These birds, so dominant during this late-winter season, will not be here for long. Within a month the fieldfares will have headed back to Scandinavia. The lapwings do not go quite so far; indeed some will travel just a short distance to Tealham Moor, bouncing around in the warm spring air during their acrobatic courtship displays.

The fields here are bounded with thorny hedgerows, studded with rows of gnarled, pollarded willows, their trunks covered with ivy. In silhouette, each is shaped like a clenched fist holding a bunch of twigs – a characteristic feature of the landscape right across the Somerset Levels.

A little further along the lane, I stumble across a scene of pure carnage. A line of willows, each reduced to a crude, bare stump, the cut wood glowing with the freshness of the sap, its grain shading from off-white to a yellowish-brown. All around, there are untidy piles of withies – the long, slender twigs of the willow – while the roadway is strewn with offcuts.

This may look like an act of wanton vandalism, but the process is vital both for the continued survival of the trees themselves and to the ecology of the area. Willow trees need pollarding every two or three years to retain their shape. In a month or two the cut bark will have darkened, the new twigs begun to sprout, and the trees will once again merge back into their ancestral landscape.

Widely used in folk medicine, both to staunch bleeding and to reduce fever, the willow was once an important local crop, making a range of products from baskets to cricket bats. Most of the larger rhynes have a row of willows along their banks, and the sound of the wind blowing through their foliage may have given rise to the belief that a willow tree will follow a lone walker on a dark night, muttering to itself.

Two examples reveal the central place of willow in local culture. First the creation, in 2001, of a giant sculpture – the Willow Man – which stands in a field alongside the western side of the M5 near Bridgwater. Created by local artist Serena de la Hey, this huge, iconic figure is one of the most striking examples of public art in Britain: Somerset's very own Angel of the North. Holidaymakers caught in bank holiday traffic jams have plenty of time to admire this extraordinary figure, whose scale only becomes clear when a crow or buzzard perches on his head, revealing his true size. He is known locally, and rather irreverently, either as the Wicker Man, or simply 'Alan', after the TV presenter Alan W(h)icker.

The other unusual use of willow relates to the untimely death, in 2003, of pop star and actor Adam Faith. His wife had heard about a Somerset firm which makes wicker coffins, and arranged for Faith to be buried in one. Her unusual choice hit the headlines, and led to a surge in demand for this environmentally friendly means of interment. Today, like Somerset cider, willow is being marketed as a 'green' product, perfectly in tune with our modern, ecologically aware age.

※

FROM THE CROSSROADS on Mark Moor, the long, straight line of River Road runs southwards to the River Brue, the farthest boundary of the parish from my home. The view here is all sky and open fields, and as befits this more intensively farmed landscape there is not a lot of winter wildlife: just a few gulls loafing around in a muddy field, with a couple of crows and a buzzard.

By the junction with Tile House Road, heading westwards to Brent Knoll, a bright green sign informs me I am standing next to Brickhouse Sluice. This crosses one of the widest rhynes in the parish, New Rhyne. The metal structure of the sluice gate once again reminds me that this whole landscape was, not so very long ago, beneath the waves.

As I gaze down the length of the rhyne, a dozen or so teal catch sight of me and take off, flying 100 yards or so away from me until they feel safe. They land again on the water and look around warily, constantly alert to the possibility of danger.

The teal is our smallest duck, barely half the length of a mallard, and only a quarter of its weight. The male is a neat little bird, especially in his newly acquired breeding plumage: his green head offset by a chestnut eyepatch, mottled greyish flanks, and a narrow yellow line running down the side of his body as if carefully painted there by a human hand. The female, as with most ducks, is rather dull – or if you prefer, subtle – her buffs and browns enabling her to stay camouflaged when on the nest.

A flock of teal is, rather appropriately, known as a 'spring'; and if you have ever flushed these diminutive ducks as you walk across the boggy fields, you'll know why. Panicked into flight, they fly up into the air as if shot from a catapult, and so are coveted by wildfowlers for their speed and agility.

Further along the rhyne I notice two smaller birds, diving down into the murky water, then bobbing up again like animated corks. Even tinier than a moorhen or teal, these are our smallest waterbird, the little grebe or dabchick.

Dabchicks, as their name suggests, look rather like the offspring of a duck or moorhen; so tiny you cannot believe they are indeed full-grown. At this time of year they are greyish-brown with a fluffy white rear-end. But in a month or so they will moult into their handsome breeding garb: richer and darker, with a deep chestnut-brown neck, and the tiniest lime-green spot behind their bill, as if someone has daubed on a dash of luminous paint. This is a colour rarely seen in nature, and all the more striking for that.

At the end of River Road, by a sharp left turn towards Burtle and Glastonbury, there is a bridge over the Brue where I once disturbed a flock of goosander, our largest freshwater duck. The turning is next to a small but imposing house, which flies the Union flag, as if marking a border; which in a sense it does.

On the side of the bridge, out of sight to anyone but the curious pedestrian, a dull metal plate is fastened to the stonework by rusty screws. It reads:

IN. MEMORY OF. ALBERT E. WATTS.
WHO WAS. KILLED ON. THIS BRIDGE
NOV 18TH 1898. AGED 33.0 YEARS
LEFT. A. WIFE. AND FIVE. CHILDREN

The ragged capital letters and random punctuation suggest the plaque was made by a friend, perhaps, rather than an experienced signwriter; lending the memorial a greater degree of poignancy.

A few weeks after noticing this, I learn the true story behind it, over a pint in the White Horse Inn with Steve, a local schoolteacher. I had assumed that the unfortunate

Albert Watts had been killed while building, or perhaps repairing, the bridge; or had been the victim of an early hit-and-run accident. In one way he was: it turns out he was bashed over the head and thrown into the River Brue late one night, after a row with another villager. A young man was tried for the murder, but acquitted for lack of firm evidence. Steve tells me that years later a father and son were overheard in the midst of an intense argument, during which the son shouted at his father, 'I almost swung for you once.' Circumstantial evidence, but pretty convincing all the same.

❧

I TURN TO head home, and my eye is caught by the rapid movement of a flock of birds over the big, wide field to the north of the river. Five hundred lapwings fly up into the air, along with a dozen smaller and more streamlined birds: golden plovers. Their high-pitched calls reach me on the chilly air; an evocative, whistling sound, reminding me of days spent in some of Britain's wildest places.

Immediately something about these birds – their tautness, and close, almost uncomfortable proximity to one another – makes me guess the identity of the creature I am about to see. A moment later I pick up a dark grey shape heading off into the distance towards Glastonbury Tor, its stiff posture and shallow wingbeats belying its speed and agility. It is, as I had already guessed, a peregrine falcon, utterly ignoring the lapwings and golden plovers, and flying nonchalantly away.

It may have forgotten them, but the lapwings and plovers can still remember the peregrine. Panicked, they fly south, then back north again, hovering over the field where they have been feeding as if wondering whether to land or not. Behaving almost as a single organism, with one mind and an infinitely flexible body, the flock occasionally splits in two, before rapidly regrouping in a narrow, fluttering line. Some birds tentatively float down towards the dark earth; but the mob mentality still rules, and at the very last moment, within touching distance of the ground, they fly back up again to rejoin their companions.

This is a crucial decision. Missing out on half an hour's feeding before dusk could make the difference between surviving the night or not. But leaving the safety of the flock could bring a much more rapid death in the predator's talons.

Ten more minutes pass, and still the birds hang above the field, collectively wasting their precious energy reserves. Once again a few individuals fold their wings and begin to whiffle down; and once again they change their minds, as if they are attached to the flock by a piece of elastic, and being pulled back up against their will. I can sense their desperation to land, and spend those last few minutes of daylight feeding; but I can also feel their acute sense of fear.

I remember when peregrines first began to turn up in southern Britain in winter, and the sheer panic that ensued whenever one would appear. Only a few years later, sightings of these mighty predators had become so regular that other birds mostly ignored them. How strange birds' minds must be: imprinted to instinctively recognise and fear something they rarely see, but which may bring sudden death.

Here in the parish, where peregrines are still not a regular sight, a healthy fear remains. Yet ironically, the peregrine is long gone by now; and the lapwings and golden plovers should be going to roost for the night. If they have any sense they will fly half a mile east to Tealham Moor, where they can sit on flooded fields, safe from the local foxes. But still they stay in the darkening sky, unwilling – or unable – to make landfall.

❁

EXPERIENCES SUCH AS this – unexpected encounters where I gain a privileged insight into the lives of our fellow creatures – make me realise the advantages of spending time in one, small, bounded area. For as other naturalists have discovered before me, a single place can provide a multitude of experiences: from the commonplace to the unusual, and the whole spectrum in between.

Being in one place is also the best way to understand the passing of the seasons: not the great shifts between winter and spring, summer and autumn, which we all notice; but the tiny, subtle changes that occur almost imperceptibly, from week to week, and day to day, throughout the year.

Gilbert White, walking the lanes and footpaths of his Hampshire parish of Selborne, knew this; as did my greatest inspiration among naturalists, the poet John Clare. Clare's story has been told often enough for me not to go into much detail here: his birth and upbringing in poverty, in a Northamptonshire village at the turn of the nineteenth century; his powers of observation that enabled him to document the wildlife of his parish; and of course his extraordinary poetical gift. The naturalist James Fisher famously described Clare as 'the finest poet of Britain's minor naturalists, and the finest naturalist of Britain's major poets'.

Just as White did, and I am doing now, Clare made most of his observations in the fields, woods and byways within a mile or two of his home. When it came to natural heritage, Clare's Helpston was pretty commonplace. But that is exactly the point: places like Selborne, Helpston and my own parish may be ordinary, but like any parish in the whole of the British Isles, extraordinary events are nevertheless taking place among the local wildlife.

My favourite of Clare's many poems on nature is a modest little sonnet, entitled 'Emmonsailes Heath in Winter'. The opening lines plunge the reader straight into the landscape, as if sharing the poet's own experience:

I love to see the old heath's withered brake
Mingle its crimpled leaves with furze and ling
While the old heron from the lonely lake
Starts slow and flaps his melancholly wing,
And oddling crow in idle motion swing
On the half-rotten ash tree's topmost twig . . .

In his characteristically punctuation-free style, Clare perfectly captures a moment in time; a moment without any real drama, and yet rooted in this particular landscape. It is this 'sense of place', as one critic described it, which makes Clare's writings on nature unique.

The poem ends with a scene which I might encounter on any winter's day, here in my own parish – 'bumbarrels', incidentally, are long-tailed tits:

The fieldfare chatter in the whistling thorn
And for the haw round fields and closen rove,
And coy bumbarrels twenty in a drove
Flit down the hedge rows in the frozen plain
And hang on little twigs and start again.

Even after the long, cold spell in January, I am still seeing little flocks of long-tailed tits foraging for food along the hedgerows behind my home. These are the lucky ones; many other small birds, here and elsewhere in the country, did not survive the snow and ice. They now lie out of sight, stiff and still, their tiny corpses bearing witness to the coldest winter I have ever known.

MARCH

As a cold February gives way to a chilly March, the lighter evenings provide an extra hour of birdsong. A hesitant dusk chorus fills the heart of the village with sound, puncturing the twilight silence of the past few months.

In the churchyard, deep in the foliage of an ancient yew, a small, unassuming little bird pierces the air with its jaunty, rhythmic song. A coal tit; the monochrome cousin of the commoner and more colourful blue tits and great tits. Like the even tinier goldcrest, this is a bird that loves conifers; and like the goldcrest, the warmth and shelter provided by this ancient yew tree has been the key to its survival during the cold spell.

Beneath the yew, on the soft, spongy, newly mown grass, a song thrush tugs determinedly at a reluctant worm, finally pulling it out of the soil and swallowing it. His head is cocked to one side, as he listens to another thrush, then another, and yet another, echoing away into the distance.

I walk past the church door, guarded by two ancient, coppery-coloured lions, flecked with lichens. So far the only flowers I can see are those placed neatly on the graves; although clumps of green daffodil shoots have begun to sprout in the spaces between the stones.

Then I find what I've been looking for. On the far side of the churchyard, jammed tight against the red brick wall of the old schoolhouse, is a single clump of greyish-green stalks, each holding a white, drooping flower. Snowdrops have finally come into bloom – almost a month later than usual.

For me, snowdrops always mark that strange no-man's-land between winter and spring. This is a time when the redwings still gather to feed in the muddy field by Mill Batch Farm, and clumps of starlings fly overhead each evening, towards their winter roost. Yet the days are beginning to lengthen, the grass is a little greener, and we wait expectantly for the first signs of migrant birds returning from Africa.

It is now a full month since the festival of Candlemas, 2 February, the date when snowdrops are traditionally meant to appear. I wonder if this will be like the seasons of my childhood: a snowy winter followed by a sudden onrush of spring, with birdsong, flowers and insects jamming up against each other in space and time. Meanwhile, I must be content with these pure white blooms, sitting chastely in a quiet corner of the churchyard.

Given our national affection for the snowdrop, it is perhaps churlish to point out that it is not actually a native plant, but was brought to Britain from southern Europe during Tudor times. Soon afterwards, in 1659, Sir Thomas Hanmer wrote this evocative description:

> The EARLY WHITE, whose pretty pure white bellflowers are tipt with a fine greene, and hang downe their heads.

Rather like the hare, another 'foreigner' we have taken to our hearts, the snowdrop always seems to me as British as any of our native plants – even more so, given its iconic status as the earliest floral harbinger of spring.

In recent years, the unprecedented run of mild winters has meant that snowdrops are often appearing at the tail end of the old year, rather than at the beginning of the new. Perhaps, in the not too distant future, they will no longer be associated with the festival of Candlemas, but with Christmas.

Mild winters have also brought plants and animals from very different seasons together, in new and unprecedented ways. A few years ago a surprising photograph appeared in the press, featuring a red admiral butterfly perched on a snowdrop. Although many people assumed it was concocted on a computer, it was indeed absolutely genuine.

Red admirals were once unknown in Britain in winter, but some now appear to be hibernating here, and will take advantage of warm, sunny days in early spring to emerge and stretch their wings. But in this, the hardest winter for at least three decades, I have yet to see a butterfly at all.

❁

WINTER MAY BE drawing to a close, but the prolonged cold spell is still taking its toll, as we discover for ourselves one bright morning. On a family walk along Perry Road, we come across the corpse of a heron, lying on the bank of the rhyne by a sharp fork in the road. There is a thin glimmer of frost on the folded wings, while the neck is bent, and the beak hidden beneath the body, as if the bird died in its sleep.

The prolonged cold, freezing the shallow water in the rhynes each night, meant that the heron was simply unable to catch enough food to replenish lost energy. Already thin – there is hardly any flesh on a heron's skeleton in the first place – it became thinner and thinner, weaker and weaker, until it could no longer summon up the energy to find its prey. Then, one cold night, it simply gave up the fight for life.

The children crowd around, fascinated, as always, by a close encounter with death. Yet all around us, as we continue along the lane, life is bursting out with the energy of spring. On the ash trees, the bare twigs are now dotted with black, sticky buds; while the laughing call of a green woodpecker echoes from the distant orchard. And even without these subtler signs, who could ignore the dozens of lambs, leaping energetically around their weary mothers in the corner field?

The bleating of the newborn lambs is the backdrop to another sound of spring: the cawing of the rooks as they spring-clean their nests in preparation for the crucial business of the breeding season ahead.

On mild, calm evenings, the rookery is full of activity. The tall ash trees at the bottom of my garden are studded with angular black shapes, a dozen in all, perched high in the twigs above their untidy nests. The hour before dusk is a time for social interaction, and they chatter noisily to one another as if recounting the day's gossip. Earlier in the day, they gathered in large, loose flocks, flapping their long, ragged wings, as they fed in the parish fields, just as they do all over rural Britain.

The rook's closest relative, the carrion crow, is by contrast a solitary bird, seemingly content with its own company. Indeed the term 'scarecrow' is a misnomer: the device was invented to scare off marauding flocks not of crows, but rooks, intent on stealing the farmer's precious seed.

Two fields away from the rookery, on the west side of Perry Road, a pair of carrion crows is sitting in the big oak; one carrying a long twig in its bill. I watch with interest, wondering if the bird will take it to its nest in the upper branches of a nearby tree, and weave it into the structure.

Instead, to my surprise, he flies away from both the tree and his mate, and lands near the edge of the field. It is only when the female flies off to join him that I understand what is going to happen. I am about to witness one of the most intimate moments in the lives of these big black birds.

As she lands, he offers the twig to her. Feigning indifference, she turns her body away from him; but then lifts her tail. It is the signal he was hoping for. Frantically flapping his wings with what looks like a mixture of sexual anticipation and triumph – but might simply be a device to keep his balance – the male crow mounts the female, and they begin to copulate.

Some half a minute later, he flies up in the air and lands a few feet away. Given that for some songbirds, mating lasts only a fraction of a second, I am impressed by his persistence. The two birds face away from each other; he digging his beak into the earth, she simply staring into space.

I am trying hard not to find human parallels in the scene I have just witnessed. Although I know this is simply instinctive behaviour, something about it seems eerily familiar. And just as with our own sexual act, this messy coupling is absolutely crucial to the crows' lives.

Two hundred yards to the east, the rooks carry on chattering to one another, too busy to notice.

❁

IN GARDENS THROUGHOUT the village, including my own, a far less conspicuous bird is also getting ready for the breeding season party. The dunnock is the wallflower of garden birds: ever-present, but hardly ever noticed. When seen at all, it is often mistaken for a sparrow; indeed the dunnock used to be known as the 'hedge sparrow', even though it is totally unrelated to the sparrow family.

Dunnocks usually forage on the ground, hopping about beneath bushes and shrubs, rather like tiny thrushes. A closer look reveals a subtle but attractive plumage: a purplish-grey head, neck and breast; with streaks of chestnut and black on the back and wings; and a slender bill, ideal for feeding on tiny insects.

For most of the year, the dunnock lives up to its reputation as a quiet, modest little bird. But for a month or two during the early spring, it undergoes a Jekyll and Hyde transformation. Gone is the shy skulker; welcome instead to the swinger of the bird world.

It starts, sometime in late January, with the occasional snatch of song, though the dunnock is never going to win any prizes for singing. Indeed it often takes a while for this stream of notes, neither high nor low, varied nor sweet, and with no clear start or finish, to permeate my consciousness.

By March, the chorus of dunnock song is building to a climax, as the males seek out high perches from which to broadcast their message. It is as if the bird, hesitant at first, has finally gained the confidence to shout to the world – or, at least, to any male or female dunnocks within earshot.

And in this village at least, there are plenty of those. Dunnocks, like many garden birds, find our shrubberies and flower beds an ideal substitute for their ancestral woodland home; and as a result, breed in far higher densities here than in their natural habitats. This leads to one of the most extraordinary displays of behaviour in the whole of the bird world, involving more extra-marital affairs than a TV soap opera.

Like all birdsong, that of the dunnock serves two purposes: to attract a mate and to drive off rival males.

But whereas most birds, once paired up, can afford to relax a little, the dunnock must keep a close eye on his mate until all their eggs have been laid. This is because female dunnocks are, to put it bluntly, fond of a bit on the side. Given the chance, they will mate with any male in the neighbourhood, and as a result any one brood of chicks in a dunnock's nest may come from several different fathers.

Not that the male is entirely blameless. He, too, hedges his bets, mating with as many females as he can find during this crucial period. Again, this maximises his chances of having the greatest possible number of chicks, and passing on his genes to future generations.

To guard against her infidelity, a male will follow his mate around as she feeds, to make sure she doesn't hop over the fence and find another male. He also copulates with her constantly – as often as a hundred times a day – although each act lasts only a fraction of a second. More extraordinary still, before this brief act of lovemaking the male will peck at the female's cloaca – the opening just beneath her tail – and remove any parcel of sperm left by a rival.

For our Victorian ancestors, such shenanigans would have seemed utterly bizarre. Not only did they believe that most birds were faithful to their partners, they even held up the dunnock as the epitome of modesty. The Reverend F. O. Morris, author of a very popular book on British birds, was especially assiduous in recommending that his parishioners should follow the dunnock's example in their marital lives. If he knew what was going on in my garden, he would surely have changed his mind.

❀

MEANWHILE, THE WAITING game continues. As the vernal equinox approaches, marking the date when the sun's favours shift from the southern to the northern hemisphere, people all over Britain are expectantly awaiting a sign – any sign – that marks the arrival of spring. For some this is the sight of a bumblebee lumbering through the air; for others, the colourful wings of an early butterfly – a brimstone, peacock or small tortoiseshell – taking advantage of the first warm, sunny day of the year.

In our village, washed by winds from the Atlantic, we enjoy a milder climate than most of the country. So our bumblebees and butterflies sometimes emerge as early as the middle of February. But after a really hard winter they stay put for much longer; the bees curled up tight in their log-pile, the butterflies hidden away in the corner of one of the many sheds, barns and outhouses dotted around the parish. Warmth is the key to their appearance: as soon as the temperature rises, and the sun shines, they will emerge to feed. But for the real stars of the spring show, another factor is just as crucial: light.

In the brains of billions of birds wintering south of

the equator, a chemical change is now being triggered – a change that will make them feel restless and uneasy. It was a German scientist who named this *Zugunruhe*. This can be translated as 'migratory restlessness': the impulse to travel vast distances across the surface of the earth, to reach their natal home.

So even now, as I listen to the resident chorus of tits and finches throughout the parish, many thousands of miles to the south a mass movement is just beginning. Even the phrase 'mass movement' seems inadequate, for this is the greatest natural phenomenon on earth. Not just tens or hundreds of millions, but *billions* of migratory birds are involved. Swallows and martins, chats and cuckoos, warblers and flycatchers, are all embarking on their epic journeys, heading back to the vast Eurasian land mass from their winter quarters in Africa.

Like some massive, unseen wave of energy, they pulse slowly across the surface of the globe towards us. With such vast numbers involved, it is easy to forget that each bird is an individual, undertaking an extraordinary journey; a journey many will fail to complete.

Predation, heat, cold, storms and sheer exhaustion are just a few of the ways a bird may meet its death while on migration: a falcon powering down out of the blue, sinking its talons into soft feathers and flesh; rain battering onto delicate wings, forcing the bird down into the sea; or simply a failure to get enough to eat, to replenish lost energy resources expended during this epic flight.

But for those birds that survive all the hazards the journey can throw at them, and do make it through, there is a prize at the end of the journey. They have won the chance to breed and raise a family, in the barns of the parish farms, under the eaves of the houses by the village hall, or in the tall ash tree at the bottom of our garden.

Now, in every village, town and city in Britain, far beyond our shores, throughout Europe and Asia, and across the Atlantic Ocean in North America, we await the return of the first migrant. It is this single, precious encounter between human and bird that will, for tens of millions of us, mark the exact moment when the cold, grim northern winter finally gives way to the warmth and joy of spring.

❀

A MONTH OR so ago, that crucial chemical trigger went off in the brain of a small, sleek, swallow-like bird, as it swooped down to feed on insects beside an African waterhole. Soon afterwards, it left behind the elephants, zebras and other big game, and headed northwards.

By mid-March this little bird had passed over the jungles of Central Africa, flown across the Sahara Desert (stopping every now and then to grab precious fuel in the form of flying insects), and then crossed the Mediterranean Sea, eventually reaching the shores of the English Channel. Here it now waits, checking the skies for the right weather conditions to fly across this short stretch of water. Very soon, around the time of the spring equinox, it and its travelling companions will finally reach our shores, and the sanctuary of their summer home.

The bird is a sand martin: the smaller, browner relative of the more familiar swallow and house martin. Not much more than 4 inches long, and weighing barely half an ounce, the sand martin is among the first migrants to return each spring. Given that it feeds exclusively on flying insects, this has always seemed a bit of a mystery to me; but the key to the sand martin's survival is that it lives and breeds near water, making its nest in holes in the sandy banks of rivers or gravel diggings.

As soon as sand martins arrive they make straight for lakes and reservoirs. Here they can replenish their energy levels, by feeding from dawn to dusk on the tiny aerial plankton which float unseen above the surface of the waves. And so I too have travelled a few miles to the north, to a vast, round bowl of water in the shadow of the Mendip Hills: Cheddar Reservoir.

The scene is remarkably spring-like, as families, accompanied by noisy children and even noisier dogs, wander around the perimeter while the sun glints off the surface of the water. The winter population of ducks, coots and other waterfowl has dropped from a few thousand at its peak to a few hundred now; though the usual gaggle of mallards remains, jostling to be the first to grab morsels of bread thrown from the bank.

And yet, despite the apparently perfect conditions, there are still no sand martins. Perhaps they have been held up by bad weather further south; or perhaps the skies are so clear that they have pressed on further north. I recall the last time I came here in March to see them, on a grey, blustery day, when several hundred of these sleek little birds were feeding low over the water.

❀

DAYS PASS, AND still no spring migrants have arrived. Frustrated with waiting, I head out to Tealham Moor, a mile or so south-east of the parish. This is the finest wildlife site within easy reach of my home: a carefully managed patchwork of grassy meadows, flooded in winter and damp in summer. Intelligent planning has created a replica of how the whole of the Somerset Levels must have looked in our grandparents' day.

A long, straight road runs east to west across the moor, rising only 2 or 3 feet above the surrounding fields. This extra height is crucial, for those fields are currently awash with a thin layer of water; in some places a foot deep. Using the car as a hide, I drive slowly along, stopping occasionally to scan with my binoculars.

The flat, silver surface of the water is broken by tight green clumps of rushes, not yet in flower; and little blades of spring grass, poking through to reach the sunlight above. This is ideal for a host of freshwater waders, including the glossy and extrovert lapwing. The air echoes with their early-spring calls, as they tumble across the sky in their elaborate courtship displays. One lapwing has a brief spat with a nearby redshank, another wader which has already begun to defend its watery territory here.

Among the lapwings and redshanks are a score of black-tailed godwits; tall, rangy wading birds, standing ankle-deep in the water. Some are asleep, heads tucked beneath their wings; others probe into the mud with their long, slightly upturned bills. They are accompanied by a pair of dunlins, and four golden plovers, one of which has already acquired his smart breeding dress of jet-black and spangled gold.

Most of the godwits are still in winter plumage, a muddy, greyish-brown shade. But a few are already beginning to moult into their splendid summer garb, suffusing their head, neck and back with a deep, rich shade of pinkish-orange. Black-tailed godwits do not breed here on Tealham Moor; indeed only a handful of pairs breed in Britain at all. These birds are heading back north to Iceland, where they nest on flower-filled meadows against a backdrop of glaciers, taking advantage of the long hours of summer daylight to raise their family.

At the back of the moor, in the deeper part of the water, several hundred wigeon are bobbing about in the water, dipping their heads down to nibble the sweet grass.

They, too, are passing through on their way north; in their case, to Siberia. But still no true spring migrants – long-distance travellers from Africa.

Then, just as I am about to leave, I notice a small movement much closer to me. By the edge of the road, dwarfed by an accompanying swan, is a small, brown wading bird, sporting a notable black mask. A glance through my binoculars reveals a narrow yellow ring around its eye. Finally, after what seems like weeks of waiting, my first returning migrant of the year: a little ringed plover, newly arrived from the tropics of Africa.

Little ringed plovers have an iconic status among British birders, especially those of my generation. In the years after the Second World War, when the countryside was suffering so much destruction of habitat, this wader bucked the trend, colonising Britain from mainland Europe.

It did so, ironically, by taking advantage of progress. The millions of roads and homes built during the post-war economic boom required tons and tons of gravel; and this led to the digging of gravel pits, mainly around the London suburbs where I grew up. Little ringed plovers usually nest on bare riverbanks, scoured clean by winter floods, as this helps them to camouflage their eggs and chicks from predators. Gravel workings provided the perfect analogue to this natural habitat.

Soon after the little ringed plover's arrival, in 1949, the naturalist and writer Kenneth Allsop published a charming novel about them, *Adventure Lit Their Star*. He was drawn to the birds precisely because they had chosen to breed not in some remote wilderness, but in what he memorably described as 'the messy limbo that is neither town nor country'.

I grew up in that same 'messy limbo' of London's suburbia, very close to where the little ringed plover began its conquest of Britain. As a result, I developed a strong attachment to this modest bird. So encountering this returning traveller today, almost within sight of my home, is both a surprise and a joy.

❀

IN THE GARDEN, spring has arrived bang on time. The morning of the vernal equinox dawns bright, sunny and warm. Today is one of only two occasions each year when the entire globe experiences twelve hours of daylight and twelve hours of darkness – give or take the transitions at dawn and dusk. And for most of us, it marks the first day of the most exciting, jam-packed and eventful season in the calendar: spring.

To celebrate this moment of global unity in their own small way, my children have chosen to leave the comfort of the sofa and play outside, in the garden. They are astonished – as am I – by the sudden appearance of crocuses and daffodils, which seem to have sprung up overnight, as if the long spell of ice and snow just a few weeks ago never happened. Bumblebees flit from bloom to bloom, while a pair of buzzards takes advantage of the rising temperatures, and the thermal air currents they produce, to soar high into the morning sky.

But for me, this jigsaw of spring still has a few pieces missing. The swallows that chatter above next door's farmyard are still somewhere well to the south of here; as are the vast majority of other returning migrants. But one summer visitor should be here; and this morning, as I tread carefully across the dew-laden grass, I shall surely hear it.

Things might be easier if I could temporarily silence the other birds: the rooks cawing constantly from the top of the ash trees; the robins singing their sweet song, and the song thrushes their more deliberate one; the dunnocks' warble, and the blue tits' chatter.

I strain my ears – is that it? No, just another blue tit. And then, 50 yards to the east, from the far side of our neighbour's garden, the sound that, for me, marks the true arrival of spring finally reaches my ears.

Chiff-chaff-chiff-chaff-chiff-chaff . . .

Yes, it's the bird which makes identification easy by singing its own name: the chiffchaff. Chiffchaffs are one of the first migrants to arrive back here each spring, usually reaching our parish in the third week of March. They have not had as far to come as some of their cousins: their closest relative, the willow warbler, travels from the southern tip of Africa, whereas most of our chiffchaffs spend the winter in Spain, Portugal or North Africa.

Indeed in recent winters, chiffchaffs have sometimes stayed put, usually in the south-west, where milder winters mean there are still small insects to be found. But most still make the short but potentially hazardous journey from the other side of Europe; and I'm pleased that this one, at least, has made it through.

Chiffchaffs aren't the most colourful or striking of birds, being small, slender and olive-green in colour, with no obvious distinguishing field-marks. Yet for me they have a real charm, perhaps because I associate them so closely with the start of my favourite season. Within a week or two my garden – and gardens and hedgerows throughout the British countryside – will be echoing to the sound of chiffchaffs from dawn to dusk, a sound we shall continue to hear throughout spring and summer. So another piece of spring's jigsaw is firmly in place; with many more to come.

Meanwhile, the buzzards have soared almost out of sight; two brown specks hanging motionless in the clear blue sky.

✿

THE GRASS IS getting greener, the shadows are becoming shorter, and the clocks go forward tonight to mark the start of British Summer Time. I am passing through the southern part of the parish, whose wide open fields contrast with the more enclosed area around my home. Among the gulls and swans gathering in the rough pasture, I notice, in the far distance, three medium-sized brown lumps. Not clods of earth, but hares; March hares, indeed.

In this part of Somerset, you can't get away from hares. Leaping hares, boxing hares, hares with huge, floppy ears. Sadly these are not real, but either painted, sculpted or cast in bronze. If you want a picture or a paperweight, a key ring or a fluffy toy, or even a bottle of beer named after a hare, I can find you one. The real thing is a little bit trickier.

As in much of the rest of Britain, we have a glut of the hare's close relative, the rabbit. Cycling around the lanes and droves of the parish, I see them everywhere: running, sitting, lolloping . . . does any other animal, apart from the rabbit, lollop?

Now, you may be of the opinion that there isn't much difference between a rabbit and a hare – in which case you've surely never seen a real, live hare. For compared with a rabbit, a hare is a Ferrari, not a Ford Focus; a Michelangelo, not a Rolf Harris; a Pelé, not a Vinnie Jones – in short, as close to the epitome of grace, beauty and style as any wild animal has a right to be.

Even before a hare moves, its shape tells you this is no ordinary creature. As it hunches close to the ground, ears twitching, its energy is barely contained. As soon as it springs into action the sense of length is palpable: long ears, long legs and long body, which somehow all fall into proportion as the animal explodes into speed. The tail is small and dark-tipped, not like the rabbit's showy powder-puff; and the sheer power of an animal which can run almost twice as quickly as the fastest human being on earth is simply awesome.

The hare's speed is just one of its armoury of weapons against predators. Another strategy is to lie flat against the ground in a shallow depression known as a 'form'. The hare's apparent ability to vanish completely, allied to the knowledge that they don't dig burrows, led to the animal being granted magical qualities. And because, like most mammals, hares are largely nocturnal, they are not seen so often during the day. All this helps explain our long love affair with this mysterious and elusive creature.

It took me a while before I even saw a hare here in the parish. My wife Suzanne had come across them, as she drove the children to nursery along Kingsway, the long, winding road which joins the centre of the village to the A38. The children had seen them too, reporting this to me with great excitement.

But it was not until I took to my bicycle, and began to explore the back lanes behind my home where the ground rises up towards the villages of Chapel and Stone Allerton, that I finally stumbled across a group of hares. Even then, I almost cycled straight past – at first mistaking them for the usual rabbits. Once I realised what they were, though,

I was able to stalk them by crouching down behind the camber of the field.

They hid well: body flat, ears down, and stock-still, apart from a nervous twitch of their huge, brown eyes. When I finally got too close, their ears pricked up, the black tips twitching like a sprinter waiting for the starting gun. Then they were off, in an explosion of movement; from stasis to speed in a fraction of a second. I was left frustrated at the brevity of our encounter, yet also elated that I had seen them at all.

Hares are usually regarded as 'one of ours': a native animal, contrasting with the alien rabbit, which was brought to Britain for food by the Romans. Yet we now know that the hare was brought here too – probably even earlier than the rabbit, during the Iron Age. But perhaps because, unlike the rabbit, it has never reached pest proportions, we are more inclined to regard it as a true Brit.

Hares are most famous for their habit of boxing, especially on bright, cold days in early spring, earning them the unfortunate epithet 'Mad March Hare'. Like so many things about hares, we haven't got this one quite right. This is not, as is often assumed, rival males fighting over a female; but the female testing out her suitors to see if they are up to the job. As so often in nature, when it comes to courtship, it is the female's preference that matters, not that of the male.

❋

IT IS THE last day of March, exactly one quarter of the way through the year. And although a casual glance could lead you to assume that the landscape has hardly changed since the start of January, the wildlife of the parish has undergone dramatic, and in many cases life-changing, experiences.

New Year frosts, followed by January snows, February thaws and March winds, have all taken their toll. But those plants and animals which have managed to survive are now ready to embark on the roller-coaster journey of spring. During the next three months, a rush of new life will change the face of the landscape and its wildlife, as birds and mammals, flowers and insects, reptiles and amphibians, trees, mosses and lichens respond to the lengthening hours of daylight, and the growing warmth of the sun.

And of all the changes I shall witness, the next month, April, will see the most dramatic and profound.

APRIL

ON EASTER SUNDAY, the cross of St George flies proudly above the church tower, battered by a stiff north-westerly breeze. Inside the thick stone walls, the Reverend Geoffrey Fenton preaches his Easter sermon. Outside, another form of resurrection continues apace: the onslaught that is the arrival of spring.

Clear blue skies, studded with a few low clouds, belie a chill in the air as I venture outdoors for a morning bike ride with the children. The sound of what they call the 'teacher bird', the syncopated song of the great tit, permeates the landscape; competing with the trill of wrens, descant of chaffinches, and the clear, pure tones of the latest arrival, the blackcap. In a willow tree by the rhyne at the bottom of the lane, a pair of chiffchaffs is setting up territory. They flit around the pale green catkins, continually pumping their tails up and down to keep their balance.

As we head back home, the children trailing their bikes behind them, the sunlight catches a small bird as it flies low over the grassy field by Perry Road. It is a shape at once familiar, yet strangely unfamiliar, for I haven't seen it for almost half a year. It is a returning swallow: my first of the spring.

I feel almost tearful as I realise that my emotional allegiance has been transferred from another returning migrant. Having lived half my life in suburbs and cities, for me the swift was always the bird that marked the true coming of summer. But now, in my fifth year in the countryside, I have shifted my loyalty to the swallow, whose constant twittering, from April to September, provides a seasonal soundtrack to our lives here in the village.

Not that this bird intends to hang around. Its long, slender wings power it onwards, as they have for the past five thousand miles, and will do for many more. It passes low over the field by Perry Farm, before rising up into the sky to clear the farm buildings, as it heads towards the parish boundary. Within minutes it has left us far behind, crossing rural Somerset, over the Cotswold Hills, and on towards the north.

Years ago, I stood on the volcanic island of Surtsey, off the south coast of Iceland, an island so new that it didn't even exist when I was born. As I tried to come to terms with this disconcerting notion, I saw a swallow hawking for insects under sunny blue skies. It was a true pioneer – swallows do not even nest in Iceland – pushing the boundaries of its range to seek out new places to live and breed.

Over the years I have watched swallows crossing the Sahara Desert in Morocco, and the Negev Desert in Israel; alongside big game in the Masai Mara and Okavango Delta; at Cape May in New Jersey, and Punta Tombo in Patagonia. In all these far-flung places I have experienced the same sense of wonder. How can this tiny bird, weighing barely half an ounce, cross the world's continents with such ease?

That same wonder grips me today, long after the swallow has flown out of sight; and I await with delicious anticipation the return of 'our' swallows, currently somewhere to the south. One day, during the next week or two, I shall hear that familiar twitter, as they swoop down to land on the telegraph wires beside our home.

Later that day, as I collect the Sunday papers from the village stores, I mention my swallow; and am told that Mrs Puddy has beaten me to it, having seen her first swallow here on the first day of the month.

❀

AT QUARTER PAST six – after dawn, but before the sun has risen above the horizon – the yaffling call of a green woodpecker echoes across a landscape draped in mist. The distant Mendips are only just visible, and a thin veil of grey covers the sky, as a shapely half-moon struggles to break through.

Rabbits skitter across the dew-drenched village lawns, while wood pigeons, disturbed by my passing, launch themselves into the cool, thin air. Like an overweight diver rashly attempting a leap from the high board, one plummets headlong towards the earth, yet just manages to avoid crashing, rising back into the air with a noisy clatter of wings.

As the moon climbs in the strengthening blue sky, a hidden blackcap is in full voice, its fluty song rippling out across the landscape to signal its return. I often wonder, if we heard the blackcap's song more regularly, whether we might rate it even higher than the usual leaders in the hit parade of British birdsongs, the blackbird and song thrush.

Meanwhile, in the centre of the village, as early-morning commuters stop off to pick up their daily newspapers, the telegraph wires hum expectantly. Throughout the winter they have borne the weight of jackdaws, starlings and collared doves – hefty birds all, causing the wires to bow heavily.

Today, a smaller, lighter burden will finally make landfall. Since that first sighting a few days ago, I have seen several swallows in the skies over the village; birds passing through on their way further north. But this morning, as I cycle beneath the wire that crosses the road between the Pack Horse Inn and Avery's Garage, I notice a small, slender bundle of feathers perched there. The first of our own swallows is back.

This bird may be alone today, but within a week others will arrive, and soon settle down to breed. All over the British countryside, from Scilly to Shetland, swallows are returning to their ancestral homes: for not only do these little birds perform the miracle of travelling all the way to Africa and back, they also manage to navigate to the very place where they were born. Such skills are almost beyond our powers of imagination, though not beyond our ability to wonder.

But these birds' stay with us is all too brief. Much sooner than we imagine, in late August and early September, they and their offspring will gather again on these same wires, this time chattering rather than silent, as if discussing the best route to take on their journey south. Then, at some unseen signal, they will head off on that epic journey: across Europe, the Mediterranean and the Sahara Desert, over the tropic of Cancer, the equator, and the tropic of Capricorn, all the way to southern Africa. But for the moment, this solitary bird perches discreetly on the telegraph wire, ignored by busy passers-by on their way to work.

❀

EACH DAY NOW, in woods, hedgerows and gardens throughout the parish, and right across Britain, one of the most extraordinary natural phenomena in the world is occurring. The dawn chorus is in full swing. Yet because it reaches its peak around daybreak, most of us are too lazy to get out of our beds to witness it.

Here in the Somerset countryside, the earliest bird is not usually the blackbird, as in more wooded parts of Britain, but the rook. Shortly before the sun begins to glow in the eastern sky, their harsh croaks can be heard from the tops of the tall ash trees dotted around the village centre. Soon afterwards, the rooks are joined by the soft, repetitive cooing of wood pigeons, and then by the first true songbirds: the delicate, plaintive lilt of the robin, and the stronger, deeper tones of the blackbird.

The traditional harbinger of daybreak, the cockerel, often wakes up later than his wild relatives. He is sometimes beaten to it by the peacocks kept by one of our neighbours, whose haunting cries pierce the cool morning air, lending an oddly exotic ambience to this very English scene.

Half an hour after the chorus begins, it accelerates, both in variety and volume. Other resident species – dunnock, wren and song thrush – start up, swiftly followed by great tits and blue tits. The first migrant to sing is, appropriately, the earliest to arrive, the chiffchaff; soon followed by the sweeter tones of the blackcap. Half an hour after sunrise, almost all the local birds have joined in, creating a wall of sound from which it can often be difficult to pick out individual species, let alone a particular songster. Finally, the finches bring up the rear, along with the distant, laughing call of a green woodpecker.

At this stage I stop bothering to try to identify every bird, and instead am content to let the chorus flow over me, like a wave surging up a beach. Hearing the whole orchestra in full flow, it is easy to forget the true purpose of this springtime phenomenon. The birds are neither trying to entertain us, nor to compete with the other species singing around them. Instead they are singing for two very specific biological reasons: to attract a mate, and to repel rival males, of the same species. So although we hear up to twenty different songs, the birds only listen to their own kind, in a kind of avian audio apartheid.

As I stand and listen, though, I can't help but ignore this, and simply revel in the privilege of being able to witness one of the greatest natural wonders in the world. What is so extraordinary is that it takes place all over Britain, from the most far-flung islands to the heart of our cities. And yet by the time we 60 million Britons have stirred from our beds, the show's over.

❀

DURING THIS SEASON, and indeed at most other times of year, the vast majority of our encounters with wildlife are with birds. And yet there are probably as many mammals as birds in the British countryside. But because so many of them are nocturnal, or simply very good at keeping hidden, we hardly ever see them. When we do, the meeting between us is often so brief that we rarely get any real sense of their lives.

Take the field vole. This is not simply the commonest mammal in Britain; it is also, with upwards of 75 million individuals, the only one to outnumber the human population of these islands.

To have a chance of finding a field vole at all, we need to resort to the rather underhand method of catching them. Fortunately Alison, a stalwart of the Mammal Society, lives along the Yarrow Road less than a fifteen-minute walk from my home. She has kindly agreed to bring along her collection of traps, hopefully to reveal the secrets of those mysterious creatures known as 'small mammals', including mice and shrews as well as voles.

One fine April evening Alison and her nine-year-old twins Lewis and Harriet pay us a visit, to set the traps. The mechanism is wonderfully simple: once the creature has run along the narrow tunnel, lured by the presence of seeds (for voles and mice) and blowfly larvae (for the insectivorous shrews), a trap door shuts behind it, so it cannot escape. Inside, it is more like a hotel than a cage: packed with straw for them to keep warm, and plenty of food, as these tiny creatures must eat almost constantly, devouring their body weight every single day, or they will die.

We spend an entertaining half-hour placing the traps in suitable locations where a small mammal might stumble across them, gaining scratched hands from the many brambles around the edges of our garden in the process. Alison warns us that we might return the next day to find all seventeen traps empty – the process is very hit and miss. But for me, that's all part of the fun.

Bright and early the following morning we are up, dressed and ready for our mammal encounters. The children are suitably excited, and I worry about how soon they might get bored if we have no luck. But of the first three traps we check, two of the doors are shut, a good sign; although rain, slugs and bad luck can all cause the door to close without a mammal inside.

Alison tips up the trap and empties what appears to be an entire haystack into a large polythene bag. There are animal droppings, then chopped pieces of grass . . . then, finally, a small, round, furry creature falls unceremoniously into the bottom of the bag. It is definitely a vole, but which one? Bank voles are a possibility – Alison often catches these in her own garden – but they have a more russet tinge to their plumage than this little beastie. Then we see the tail; or, at least, what there is of it: a short, stumpy protuberance, only an inch or so long. This, together with the greyish-brown fur, confirms that this is indeed a field vole.

After all the children have taken a good look at the animal, Charlie is chosen to release it. As soon as the vole lands on the ground it disappears into the long grass, melting away, before surfacing again a foot or so further along; then with two or three short, jerky hops, it is gone.

We also strike lucky with the next trap: another field vole, swiftly followed by a third. And at the bottom of the garden, two more rodents: smaller and more slender, white below and yellowish-brown above, with long, oval-shaped ears. These are wood mice: the quintessential wild mouse of our countryside.

When released they dash away even more quickly than the voles, this time on the surface of the grass rather than burrowing underneath. The second mouse entertains the children by momentarily dancing across their wellington boots; a second later it has also disappeared.

Over a cooked breakfast, the children chatter excitedly about their experience. They, and we, will never look at our back garden in quite the same way again.

※

TWO ROADS – ONE ancient, one modern – skirt the north-western boundary of the parish. The more obvious of the two is the M5, whose six carriageways weave across the flat landscape on its journey south from Birmingham to Exeter. This is the main holiday route to and from the south-west, bringing hordes of holidaymakers from the Midlands to the nearby beach resorts of Burnham-on-Sea and Weston-super-Mare. The latter seaside town is known affectionately as 'Weston-super-mud', due to the sea's extraordinary tidal range here.

Shadowing the motorway is a much older road: the A38, which has been described as 'the longest country lane in England'. It may be smaller and quieter than its six-lane counterpart, but it is almost twice as long, running for more than three hundred miles from Bodmin Moor in Cornwall, to Mansfield in the heart of the East Midlands.

If you are stuck in bank holiday traffic on either road, it is always worth looking out for wildlife. And today, in the shadow of Brent Knoll, a slender, long-winged creature hangs motionless, some 30 feet above the hard shoulder. It is a kestrel: the classic bird of our motorway system; though now, sadly, a far less frequent sight than it used to be.

When I was growing up, the kestrel was by far our most common bird of prey, but it is now down to third place, behind the buzzard and the sparrowhawk. These are enjoying a population boom, while the kestrel is currently the only British raptor in decline. This may be to do with a shortage of its favourite food, the field vole; another casualty of modern farming.

I watch as the bird performs its hunting ritual, hovering motionless – apart from its winnowing wings – for a few seconds, before dipping one wing in order to change position and begin hovering again. Slow-motion film has revealed that although the hovering kestrel makes constant tiny adjustments to the position of its body and wings, its eyes stay locked in place, focused intently on the ground below. The bird is searching for the tiny movements which will reveal the presence of a vole.

The kestrel also has a secret weapon. As field voles swarm through the dense grassy verges, they leave a constant trail of urine to mark their tiny territories. But this convenient messaging service has deadly consequences. The urine is visible in ultra-violet light; and kestrels, like other birds, are able to see light at wavelengths invisible to us. So the hovering kestrel isn't simply watching for the voles to move, but can also follow their telltale urine trails, and use these to locate its prey.

Once it has spotted the vole, the kestrel folds up its wings in an instant and drops like a stone to the ground, feet first, to grab the unsuspecting rodent in its needle-sharp talons. Using this hovering technique to hunt may be highly effective, but it also takes up precious energy resources. So during the winter months these little falcons employ a different strategy. Instead of hovering, they perch on the many telegraph poles that line the back lanes of the parish, and simply drop down onto their prey.

The kestrel's main hunting method gave it the folk name 'windhover', made famous by the nineteenth-century Jesuit priest and poet Gerard Manley Hopkins. Characteristically, the rhythm of the verse appears to mimic the actual movement of the bird:

> *I caught this morning morning's minion, king-*
> *   dom of daylight's dauphin, dapple-dawn-drawn*
> *   Falcon, in*
> *   his riding*
> *Of the rolling level underneath him steady air, and*
> *   striding*
> *High there, how he rung upon the rein of a wimpling*
> *   wing*
> *In his ecstasy! Then off, off forth on swing,*
> *   As and gliding a skate's heel sweeps smooth on a*
> *   bow-bend: the hurl*
> *   and gliding*
> *   Rebuffed the big wind.*

Dedicated 'to Christ our Lord', the poem is perhaps the best-known example in the English canon of a wild creature being used as a religious image. But whatever your own beliefs, surely no one can fail to be stirred by the sheer energy and power of the verse.

As a devout Catholic, Hopkins might have been shocked by an even older name for the kestrel: the wind fucker, as in this observation from the late sixteenth century:

> *The kistrilles or windfuckers that fill themselues with winde, fly against the winde euermore.*

In *The Oxford Book of British Bird Names*, Professor W. B. Lockwood discusses the origins of this apparently vulgar folk name. He explains that when it was first used, at the turn of the seventeenth century, the word was only just beginning to acquire its modern connotations. So it is simply being used in its original sense, meaning 'wind beater'.

But whatever we call this stunning bird, for the next few months, motorists here and across the whole of the country will enjoy a fleeting glimpse of this most effective hunter, hovering above the byways and trunk roads of lowland Britain.

❀

I HAVE, ON my bookshelf, a small, squat volume entitled *A Field Guide to Birds' Nests*. Published in 1972, and written by the late Bruce Campbell and the doyen of living ornithologists, James Ferguson-Lees, it has long been out of print. Which is a pity, for this is the bible of the long-forgotten art of nest-finding; a skill that, having been built up over hundreds of years, vanished in a couple of decades. This was thanks to the Bird Protection Acts, which meant the death knell for egg-collecting.

Of course, collecting birds' eggs is not only illegal, it is immoral too. To interfere with nature's most important process – the ability of a wild creature to pass on its genes to future generations – is not something anyone can or should condone. Thanks to our bird protection laws, egg-collecting is now dead and buried, apart from a tiny hard core of obsessive and misguided individuals who continue to rob the nests of rare birds.

But sadly, the opprobrium heaped on egg-collecting had unintended consequences for the innocent pastime of finding birds' nests. This now is not just deeply unfashionable, but has disappeared off the radar of almost all birders and naturalists, including myself.

It wasn't always so. Mine was the last generation of schoolboys who dabbled in the dark arts of nest-finding. I can still remember my sheer joy on discovering a song thrush's nest, complete with its clutch of sky-blue eggs speckled with black. Most years a blackbird would nest in the thick clematis by our kitchen window; while great tits would regularly occupy the nestbox I put up by the pear tree.

Later on, I would search the edges of the gravel pits near my home, looking for the nests of coots, swans and great crested grebes. The grebes would build a low, floating platform out of aquatic vegetation, which always appeared empty. But closer inspection would reveal a clutch of three or four elongated eggs, carefully hidden under a layer of water-weed, staining them pale green.

Now, armed with my little guidebook, I am determined to relearn the skills I had as a child; and rediscover the joys of 'birds-nesting', as it used to be called. I get the opportunity to do so sooner than I thought. Blackbirds usually build their nests in dense foliage, so when I disturb a female in the upper floor of one of our outbuildings, I do not immediately realise the significance of her presence.

The second time this happens, as she perches on the brickwork and chatters frantically at me, I realise there must be a reason why she does not immediately fly away. Then, an arm's-length in front of me, I notice an untidy nest, jammed against one of the roof beams. I tentatively feel inside the cup, and there, nestled among a lining of mud and fine grass, is a clutch of five eggs. They are warm to the touch, so I rapidly retreat, allowing the female to resume her incubation duties.

Our workshop, where the blackbird has chosen to breed, is unexpectedly popular this year, with baby robins emerging from the back door, and a pair of blue tits nesting in a gap by the outflow pipe of the washing machine. Given the availability of natural sites, and the many nestboxes I have put up around the garden, it seems perverse that they should choose such peculiar places to raise a family. But it is also comforting that these wild creatures should make their home in ours.

❀

SOME TIME AROUND the middle of April, earlier in some years than others, a ridge of high pressure builds out in the Atlantic Ocean, blocking the usual series of depressions that sweep up the Bristol Channel and over our heads. Clear skies bring chilly nights, and the risk of frost for the village gardeners. But once the sun is up, the days turn warm and pleasant; and each evening, drinkers sit outside the White Horse Inn enjoying a pint, and the unexpected feeling of spring sunshine on their faces.

High above them, in the clear blue sky, millions of tiny insects buzz unseen, like plankton floating in the vast expanse of the ocean. And into this sea of blue sails a creature: dark blue-black above, snow-white below, uncannily reminiscent of a killer whale.

Like the killer whale it is an extraordinary traveller; capable of covering thousands of miles on its global journeys. Unlike the killer whale, it weighs less than an ounce, making its voyaging and navigational abilities even more impressive. It is a house martin, whose slender, streamlined body cuts easily through the cool air, its beak hoovering up the tiny insects it uses to fuel its passage.

I'd like to tell you where it has come from, but the truth is we have very little idea where house martins spend their time when they are away from our shores. We do know that they head somewhere south of the equator. Yet of more than 300,000 house martins ringed in Britain in the past hundred years or so, just one has been 'recovered' – trapped again or found dead – on its wintering grounds.

The maths is sobering: twenty million European breeding pairs and their young – upwards of a hundred million birds in all – more or less disappear, with only small numbers being seen at scattered locations around the continent. Some have speculated that they live high above the densest jungles, feeding on insects dislodged by heat or forest fires; others that they fly low over the open savannah. But whatever the truth, the paradox remains: how can a bird so familiar that we name it after our homes (and the French after their windows – *hirondelle de fenêtre*) vanish so effectively for half its lifespan?

The bird's scientific name, *Delichon urbicum*, is both an academic joke and a misnomer: *Delichon* is an anagram of the Greek word for swallow, *Chelidon*; while *urbicum* refers to the bird's supposedly city-dwelling habits. In fact this name would be better applied to the true bird of summer in the city, the swift; for the house martin is primarily, in England at least, a bird of small towns and villages.

Of course this cannot always have been so. Like the

house sparrow, the house martin must once have nested in natural structures. A few years ago, while walking along a beach in West Wales, I discovered three or four mud nests, carefully constructed under the overhang of a cliff. If cliffs and caves were its only dwellings, the house martin must have been a scarce bird before we came along, as there would have been far fewer sites where it could nest.

Shakespeare not only knew the house martin, but mentioned it in one of his most memorable passages, in *Macbeth*. The lines are uttered by the doomed Banquo, as he arrives at the castle near which he will meet his terrible fate. But for the moment, at least, all is fine with the world:

> *This guest of summer,*
> *The temple-haunting martlet, does approve,*
> *By his loved mansionry, that the heaven's breath*
> *Smells wooingly here: no jutty, frieze,*
> *Buttress, nor coign of vantage, but this bird*
> *Hath made his pendent bed and procreant cradle:*
> *Where they most breed and haunt, I have observed,*
> *The air is delicate.*

Sadly the air is no longer so delicate for the house martin, whose fortunes are now on a downward path. In my own lifetime I have seen this familiar summer visitor disappear from many of its former haunts; perhaps as a result of hostile householders who don't want to be woken at dawn by the cries of hungry chicks. Personally, I can't imagine a better way to start a summer's day.

❊

AROUND THIS TIME of year, another seasonal sound fills the air: the noise of dozens of lawnmowers being fired up for the first time since the previous autumn. Birdsong is temporarily blotted out, as this metal army wreaks havoc across the village lawns, large and small.

Daisies and dandelions, which for a week or two have carpeted the grass with yellow and white, are hacked down in their prime by the mowers' blades. By late afternoon, the air of this and a thousand other parishes is filled with the heady scent of new-mown grass; which smells, oddly, rather like a good Sauvignon Blanc.

The rising temperatures have brought another mass emergence: as two small insects, one orange and black, the other orange and white, take to the air. They are the comma and the orange-tip butterflies, both classic signs of spring.

The comma, named after the small white marking on its dark underwings, is one of a handful of British butterflies to overwinter here as adults. They hide away in garages, sheds and outbuildings, until they emerge on a fine day – some years as early as February or March; in others not until April. They remain on the wing throughout the spring and summer: their jagged wings, and bright orange-and-black markings, making them easy to pick out. Today the comma is a winner among our butterflies, having recently extended its range north to colonise Scotland. Yet bizarrely, a century ago it was one of our rarest, found only in a few places along the border between England and Wales.

The male orange-tip, too, is easy to pick out; and an even more timely sign of spring, appearing regularly as clockwork on the first warm, sunny day after the start of April. I usually find orange-tips at the bottom of our garden, where there is a healthy clump of one of their caterpillars' main food-plants, garlic mustard. Elsewhere they flit delicately along the edges of the rhynes and lanes, their bright orange wingtips flashing in the sunshine. Females are far less conspicuous, as their lack of orange wingtips suggests one of the 'cabbage whites', but a closer look reveals a delicate greenish mottling on the underside of the wings.

Their subtle beauty conceals a dark secret. Unlike most other British butterflies, female orange-tips lay their eggs singly, flitting from flower to flower and carefully depositing a tiny greenish-white egg, barely visible to the human eye, beneath the buds. This is because when the caterpillar hatches, it will eat not only the food-plant on which it has emerged, but also any other caterpillars it finds there. This cannibalistic behaviour evolved because if several caterpillars tried to live on a single plant they would starve for lack of food.

But I can forgive them for this. For me, orange-tips symbolise that brief, heady period when spring is in full flush, and all is new and fresh. By late May they have usually disappeared, their luminous wingtips but a fading memory.

❀

By St George's Day, 23 April, everything is in full swing, springwise. From dawn to dusk the parish air is filled with the sounds of birdsong. In the ragged, untidy hedgerow bordering the rhyne behind our home, two tiny brown birds are engaged in a face-off: each attempting to maintain the invisible border between their equally tiny territories.

Their song – a series of notes, trills and whistles ending with a flourish – echoes around the whole parish, and indeed the whole of the country. For the wren is not only one of the most common birds here, but the most common species in Britain; a fact that surprises many people, as sightings of this little bird can be few and far between. But like so many of our songbirds, once you become familiar with their sound, you realise they are everywhere.

I have seen and heard wrens in city gardens and along country lanes; on coastal paths and remote islands, including the larger, darker race that lives only on the remote archipelago of St Kilda. There, as waves crashed against sea cliffs and the wind whistled through the drystone walls, I watched as these testosterone-fuelled little bundles of feathers sang even more loudly than their mainland cousins, to make themselves heard above the raging of the elements.

Back here in the parish, and indeed all across the northern hemisphere, the final pieces of the jigsaw of returning migrants are being slotted into place. Just along the hedgerow, deep inside the blackthorn foliage, another small bird is singing: a nondescript, scratchy little warble, hardly audible above the rival wrens. Occasionally it reveals itself, the morning sunlight catching its plumage. It is slender and clean-lined, with a grey head, chestnut-coloured wings, and the decidedly white throat which our ancestors chose for its name.

Just last night this whitethroat – along with tens of thousands of others – took advantage of a shift from northerly to southerly winds, and flew across the English Channel. It is an early arrival, the vanguard of almost a million pairs currently returning from Africa, to breed throughout the British countryside.

Like so many of our summer visitors, the whitethroat is very vulnerable to problems on its wintering grounds, as happened in the spring of 1969, when nine out of ten birds failed to return. The cause of this sudden population crash was a prolonged drought in the Sahel Zone of West Africa, where most British whitethroats spend the winter. Whitethroats have since made a comeback; but as climate change has led to the Sahara Desert extending its boundaries, the chances of history repeating itself would appear to be high.

Another summer visitor is also singing, this time from the blossom-filled apple trees in the village's few remaining orchards. The willow warbler's song is a plaintive, silvery run of notes, descending down the scale like water trickling down a slope. It is the classic sound of the birch and willow forests of northern Europe. Here in Britain it is, surprisingly, our most frequent summer visitor; a couple of million pairs comfortably outdoing more familiar and visible migrants such as the swallow and house martin.

Like the swallow, willow warblers are true long-distance migrants, with some British birds flying as far as the Cape of Good Hope. Once, on a visit to South Africa, I heard a familiar song, and assumed it was a local species that sounded like a willow warbler – only to realise that it was, of course, the real thing.

Every spring, sometime from the middle of April onwards, a small wave of willow warblers passes through our parish; stopping briefly to sing in our gardens and orchards. But although this seems as good a place as any to breed, most leave after a few days, heading on northwards to Scotland or Scandinavia. One or two pairs do linger, and I occasionally hear them in May and June; but the less tuneful sound of their close relative, the chiffchaff, is the dominant sound of spring in these parts.

One final member of this little group of summer visitors is usually the last to arrive. Sometime during the last week of the month, a quiet, modest warble can be heard, coming from thickets of bramble and hawthorn. The sound is so tentative it almost seems as if the bird is tuning up for a proper performance later on.

The singer is a lesser whitethroat; slightly smaller than the common whitethroat, and a lot less conspicuous. Like the whitethroat, it has travelled here from West Africa, but not, as one might imagine, by the most direct route across the Sahara and western Europe. Instead, it follows its ancestral migration path, which takes it the long way round, via the Middle East and the Balkans, before finally reaching its destination. No wonder the birds in this parish, and indeed across the rest of Britain, usually arrive a few days later than the whitethroats.

❀

IN A NEIGHBOURING village, next to an ancient church-yard and rectory, stands a magnificent specimen of holm oak. Also known as the Mediterranean oak, this exotic tree was introduced from southern Europe in Tudor times, and now grows freely in the milder parts of the country, including here in the south-west. Dense and bushy, it sports dark green leaves rather like holly, and indeed shares the second part of its scientific name, *Quercus ilex*, with that plant. Its large size makes it an ideal nesting site for one of our biggest breeding birds, the grey heron.

The flapping of broad, heavy wings, and a deep, hoarse cry, signals the return of one of these great birds to its nest, high in the canopy. Herons are colonial breeders, and will return to the same tree, and indeed the same nest, year after year, simply adding a few twigs to the untidy structure in order to make repairs.

Herons are also one of our earliest nesters, and these came back in January or February, long before most birds begin to breed. So the evergreen foliage of this huge oak provides a safer home than any of our broad-leaved, native species, where the nests and eggs might be vulnerable to predators.

There is a score of heronries in the county, but this is one with a difference. For interspersed among the grey herons' nests there are a dozen or so smaller structures, belonging to their close relative, the little egret. Through the branches I can just make out that the egrets are sporting the long, feathery plumes which almost led to their downfall. Back in the nineteenth century, before the RSPB managed to stop the grisly trade, these beautiful birds were killed in their tens of thousands to fuel the demand for feathers to adorn the fashions of Victorian high-society ladies.

The egrets breed later than the herons, so while the latter are now sitting tightly on eggs, their smaller cousins are still adding extra twigs to their flimsy-looking nests. It always surprises me that such a beautiful and graceful bird should make such a raucous sound, but this simply fits the usual laws of nature: birds with a striking plumage do not need a fine song, and vice versa. Just compare the kingfisher and nightingale.

I am visiting the heronry with David, a retired schoolmaster of the traditional kind. He is the sort of man by whom I would have enjoyed being taught, with just the right mixture of knowledge and enthusiasm. David is the acknowledged authority on the history of Somerset's birds, and over many years has charted their fortunes with characteristic attention to detail.

The purpose of our visit is to count the nesting herons for the BTO's annual census, the longest-running survey of a single species anywhere in the world. It was begun in 1928, by the great ornithologist Max Nicholson, and continues throughout Britain to this day. So it is that, more than eighty years after that first national count, David and I are peering through the foliage to try to ascertain how many nests there actually are. We find three, and are relieved that there are any at all, after the hardest winter for a generation, which killed off many herons here and elsewhere in the country.

❦

BACK IN THE depths of that bitter winter, Tealham Moor was both beautiful and virtually lifeless. Beautiful, because plummeting temperatures had fixed the fluid, watery landscape into a permanent vision of white. A layer of ice had hardened the surface of the rhynes, and turned the water meadows into a skating rink, while a wafer-thin layer of frost coated every hedgerow, bush and blade of grass.

Lifeless, because with access to the water denied, the thousands of birds that usually feed here had fled south and west in search of ice-free landscapes. Only a single, solitary bird, a reed bunting, flitted along the edge of the frozen rhyne, in a vain attempt to find something – anything – to eat.

Now, towards the end of April, the scene has been utterly transformed: for with water and sunshine comes life. Skylarks sing their aerial song for hours on end, kestrels hover in search of voles, and dozens of mute swans graze the meadows. Meanwhile lapwings and redshanks perform their noisy aerial displays in the sky, above their tight clutches of eggs, safely hidden in the long grass below.

In a poll to find the most handsome wader in Britain, the lapwing would be hard to beat. At a distance, as they fly acrobatically above the wet meadows of the moor, they appear black and white. But when they land they reveal their true colours. As on an artist's palette, these are not distinct, but a swirling mixture of shades: greens, browns and purples, their edges blurring into one another, and changing as the bird turns in the spring sunlight. These are set off by bright white underparts, an orange-ochre patch beneath the tail, and that slightly comical crest, which always looks as if it has been stuck on to the bird's head as an afterthought.

The lapwing's neighbour, the redshank, is not bad-looking at this time of year either. It has changed from the dull grey-browns of winter into a fine-looking creature: dark, almost chocolate-brown, spangled with paler spots, with orange-red legs and base to its bill. When it flies, it reveals telltale white flashes along the trailing edge to the wing, which together with the three-note alarm call have earned it the nickname 'sentinel of the marsh'.

Where the lapwings and redshanks patrol along the edge of their territories, custard-yellow dandelions grow in their tens of thousands, while a more subtle plant, lady's smock, also studs the grass with its pale lilac blooms. During the ice and snow this delicate little wild flower, a cousin of the watercress, retreated into the soil; but now, with the warmer temperatures and sunshine, it has emerged to add its contribution to the beauty of the scene. The name refers to its apparent resemblance to the smocks commonly worn by country women in Tudor times; while an alternative folk name, 'cuckoo-flower', nods to its appearing at the same time as that returning bird.

Butterflies love lady's smock, as shown by the profusion of green-veined whites and orange-tips on the moor at this time of year. One green-veined white flutters on top of his mate, closing his wings to reveal the pattern beneath; delicate greenish stripes on a background of pale lemon-yellow. But he has become carried away in his eagerness to breed, and as he flies off, she remains stuck in the mud at the edge of the rhyne, vainly flapping her wings in an effort to escape.

Every now and then, a small, bright, yellow object appears to detach itself from the carpet of dandelions covering the moor, and flies through the air in a bouncing motion. The yellow wagtail is a beguiling bird, but its numbers are rapidly declining. Thanks to the wildlife-friendly farming here on the moor, a tiny population of yellow wagtails continues to find sanctuary here. Even so, they remain very vulnerable: a passing cow may tread on the nest, crushing the clutch of five or six tiny, pale buff eggs; or the dark shape of a passing merlin may grab this colourful bird clean out of the air, ending its brief life in a moment.

The male wagtail perches on a prominent twig, barely sturdy enough to bear his weight. He struggles to keep his balance in the breeze, fanning his broad tail, before flying off to grab a small insect. He always returns to the same perch, for as well as feeding, he must continue to defend his territory against incoming males.

Meanwhile a constant battle is being fought between the breeding waders and the local crows. A dark, brooding presence, they sit on fence posts around the periphery of the moor, or patrol overhead, alert to any opportunity to grab unguarded eggs. All day long, and every day during the spring, the sound of lapwings fills the air, as they try to drive away the much larger crows. In turn, the crows mob any buzzard that has the temerity to pass overhead, seeing it away with harsh, angry cries.

As a child, I remember finding a lapwing's nest on a patch of waste ground near my home in the London suburbs. I can still see the neat clutch of four pear-shaped, olive-brown eggs with dark blotches, staring up at me from the grassy tussock where they were hidden. Today, lapwings have disappeared from there, and indeed from most of the wider countryside, and breed only on nature reserves or specially managed farmland such as here on Tealham Moor.

Some might wonder why it matters that lapwings, and many other once-common farmland birds, have declined. But as well as the loss to our natural heritage, lapwings are also part of our cultural inheritance. And just as, in the words of John Donne, 'any man's death diminishes me', so the loss of the lapwing, the skylark and many other familiar birds of the British countryside diminishes us too.

❦

ANOTHER SPECIES OF wader, the whimbrel, occasionally passes through the parish on its spring migration north. This is the smaller, neater relative of the more familiar curlew, with a slightly shorter, downcurved bill, and a bold dark stripe above its eye.

One of the annual highlights here on the Somerset Levels used to be flocks of whimbrel, sometimes numbering in their hundreds, passing through at the end of April en route from West Africa to Iceland and Scandinavia. Today they still occasionally appear, but in far lower numbers than before. Their characteristic call, a rapid series of seven fluty notes, is often the first clue to the birds' presence, as they float down onto the moor to feed and rest before setting forth on their journey once again.

Very occasionally an even rarer migratory wader also stops off here. The wood sandpiper is a bird of boggy swamps of the north, nesting from Scandinavia all the way across Eurasia to Kamchatka, with a tiny population in the far north of Scotland, and wintering in sub-Saharan Africa, Asia and Australia.

The pair of wood sandpipers feeding unobtrusively on Tealham Moor on a cool, damp, spring day have come, like the whimbrel, from Africa. Sleek and long-legged, they are very attractive waders, with a pale, spangled appearance. They use their delicate, slender bills to pick off insect food as they pass across the meadow. We are lucky to see them at all: although wood sandpipers sometimes stop off here as they travel south in autumn, in spring they are in a hurry to breed, so usually fly straight overhead.

Our country is important as a transit lounge for birds like these, passage migrants, birds which neither breed nor spend the winter here, but simply stop off on their way north and south each spring and autumn. So just as we have a responsibility for our resident birds such as the lapwing and skylark, our summer visitors, the swallow and house martin, and our winter visitors, the redwing and fieldfare, so we owe these passing creatures the same duty of care. The way we farm Tealham Moor, and other places up and down the country, doesn't just benefit our local birds. It also helps those like the whimbrel and wood sandpiper, which stop off here for a few days – or even just a few hours – on their global travels.

❁

AT ABOUT THIS time of year, a far less welcome visitor turns up in the fields and gardens of the parish. It is a large, ungainly, black insect, named St Mark's fly because it generally appears on or around 25 April, the feast day of St Mark.

It is a very common sight here, swarming en masse across any area of grassland it can find, its long legs dangling as if it has forgotten to lift them up towards its body. The males can, with a good view, be told apart from the larger females by their bulbous-looking eyes, giving them a rather unbalanced, front-heavy appearance, as if they are about to crash to the ground.

Having emerged in late April, St Mark's flies usually stay around until May or June, though their numbers are depleted by the predations of birds which take advantage of this unexpected bounty of easily caught food. The flies also help to pollinate the many apple trees in the orchards of the parish, while their larvae aid the process of decomposition by feeding on decaying vegetable matter, often in compost heaps. So even though the St Mark's fly is not a particularly attractive insect, it is certainly a very useful one.

❁

ON THE FINAL day of the month, as dusk cloaks the lanes, fields and hedgerows, the air is still filled with birdsong. Above the rest of the evening chorus, one bird continues to reign supreme: the song thrush. He sits on our chimney pot, spotted breast and throat vibrating as he delivers his clear, strident and melodic tune, a full two months or more after he first began to sing.

From the garden next door, another thrush answers him, seeming to fill in the gaps in his tune with its own. To the east, south, north and west, in every corner of the parish, more song thrushes are singing too, so that the air above is filled with their sound.

Somewhere close to each singing male, a female sits tightly on her clutch of four or five sky-blue eggs, speckled delicately with tiny spots of black; those precious objects Hopkins called 'little low heavens'. Underneath her body, cosseted by her soft feathers, the eggs stay warm. Inside each egg, a tiny thrush-to-be is growing. I like to think it is listening to the muffled song of its father, high above.

MAY

M AY BEGINS, AS April ended, with the sound of
the song thrush, its clear, strident notes herald-
ing the dawn, in the few seconds the sun takes to
cross the parish from Poolbridge Farm in the east to the
Watchfield Inn in the west.

Since the May Day bank holiday was first introduced
in the late 1970s, we have come to associate it with a long
weekend off work, but its origins go much further back
in time. The pagan festivals of Flora, the Roman goddess
of flowers, and the ancient Celtic festival of Beltane, both
marked the cross-quarter day: the mid-point between the
sun's progression from the spring equinox on 21 March to
the summer solstice three months later.

For centuries the English have celebrated May Day
with a range of traditional pastimes: from maypoles and
morris dancing to the crowning of the May Queen. May
baskets of flowers used to be left on neighbours' doorsteps;
a custom echoed today in the springtime appearance of
hanging baskets on many of the village homes. And not
so long ago, farmers would have chosen this time to move
their livestock from their winter home on the surrounding
hills, along the broad, muddy droves, to graze on the
summer pastures of Tealham Moor.

We also mark this time of year because this is when we
can finally leave the memories of winter behind, and celebrate the onset of summer; though even here in the mild
south-west ground frosts can occur well into May. As is

traditional on bank holidays, we sometimes get rain, and even though this might dampen the spirits of the morris dancers, it does supposedly foretell a fertile year ahead. And the maypole itself is a symbol of fertility, both for the men and women who dance around it, and for the land.

For our parish wildlife, May is also a time of growth and fertility. It marks the start of three months of frantic activity, during which time eggs will hatch, babies will be fed, flowers will bloom, and millions – perhaps billions – of insects will buzz, bite and sting their way through their brief lives, and indeed through ours.

The weather for this month, and for June, July and August, will be crucial to the success or failure of these attempts to breed and multiply. So the wildlife, the farmers and the rest of us are all hoping for a good season – not too wet, but not too dry either, with just enough rain, and plenty of warm sunshine. This will ripen the crops, let plants and animals thrive, and allow us to sit in our gardens or stroll along the parish lanes, enjoying the great British summer to the full.

❀

ON THIS PARTICULAR May Day, I have come a few miles west of the parish, to the beach at Berrow. Showers are forecast, but for the time being a milky morning sun bathes the sand in a thin, yellowish glow. As I cross the sheltering dunes, I am buffeted by a cool, fresh breeze which blows the tidal pools into eddies, and whips up sand along the strandline.

Lying between the busy holiday resorts of Burnham and Weston, Berrow is quieter and less crowded than both, with only the occasional dog-walker, jogger or horse-rider disturbing the solitude. This is the nearest this part of Somerset gets to the seaside, though the sign warning of 'soft sand and mud', suggests that bathing here might not be a very good idea.

Beyond the sign, only a narrow strip of sand remains; sand mainly concealed by messy deposits of seaweed, driftwood, and the flotsam and jetsam of our throwaway society. As I emerge at the top of the beach I step across detritus washed up by the sea: broken branches bleached white in the sun, plastic bottles in a range of colours and shapes, and a child's trainer left behind after a day on the beach.

This is where three rivers meet. The River Brue, which runs along the southern border of my parish, joins the estuary of the Parrett, which has already wended its way forty miles north from its source in Dorset. This in turn flows into Bridgwater Bay, adjacent to the much larger estuary of England's longest river, the Severn. The mudflats provide a profitable feeding place for tens of thousands of waders at low tide, while the raised banks of Steart Point across the smaller estuary are a haven where they can safely roost as the waters rise.

At low tide the sea becomes invisible, having retreated

almost to the horizon, so that the island of Steep Holm appears to rise straight out of the land. But now, on a high spring tide, the landscape – and seascape – is transformed. Steep Holm has regained its island status, and from Hinkley Point nuclear power station on my left, to Cardiff's Millennium Stadium on my right, all is under water.

Along the shoreline, black against the pale sand, is one of the beach's permanent residents, a scavenging crow. He and the local gulls witness the seasonal movements of birds here: Arctic terns and ringed plovers in spring; gannets and Manx shearwaters in summer; clouds of knots and sanderlings in autumn; and huge, swirling flocks of dunlins in winter. Today, there are only a few late-returning swallows flying in off the sea, which apart from a hardy yachtsman taking advantage of the breeze, appears empty.

The twice-daily movement of the tides brings fresh supplies of seaweed to the higher parts of the beach, on which millions of tiny sandflies make their home. Behind the beach lie the dunes; and beyond the dunes a golf course; with a small reedbed sandwiched between. This morning, despite the grey skies and chilly breeze, the reeds and the bushes resound with birdsong, in particular the varied sounds of the warbler family: whitethroats and lesser whitethroats, blackcaps and chiffchaffs, and Cetti's, sedge and reed warblers.

❀

Back in the parish, the reeds lining the ditches on both sides of the back lanes are reaching their peak. These are the common reed, *Phragmites australis*, found in wetlands not only throughout Britain, but across much of the world; here in the parish it grows in striking profusion in every watery ditch.

The tall, thick stems, with their feathery, plumed heads, often block the view of the fields beyond the lanes, especially in spring and summer when their growth is at its most luxuriant. They sway at any hint of a breeze, and when the wind strengthens they create a pleasing background murmur. Known locally as shalders, reeds were widely used for thatching on the levels right up to the present century. Now that they are no longer harvested commercially, they are left uncut, providing the ideal habitat for a specialist wetland bird, the reed warbler.

The reed warbler is the classic 'little brown job': small, unassuming, and generally hidden out of sight in the reeds. In May and June the rhynes of the parish resound with its rhythmic and repetitive song, although I would be surprised if more than half a dozen of my fellow villagers were aware of the bird at all. Yet it has an extraordinary story to tell: of a global voyage to and from distant lands, in the very heart of Africa.

Reed warblers arrive back in Britain in the middle of April, though I rarely hear them here until the end of the month. This is when the males are seeking out their breeding territories, sometimes in a tiny patch of reeds hardly worthy of the name, where I can hear them singing from dawn until dusk.

Without their song, we would be probably not even realise they were here, for they hardly ever emerge from their hidden home. They build their nest in the reeds, expertly weaving together a neat, conical cup from strands of grass, lined with moss and feathers, attached to the stems. Into this fragile basket the female will deposit her clutch of four or five olive-coloured eggs.

Only later in the year, when the youngsters leave the safety of their nest, do I finally get a decent view of reed warblers. Even then they are not all that easy to see, as they skulk around the foliage of the bramble bushes and hedgerows, dashing back into their reedy sanctuary at the slightest sign of danger.

❈

WHAT STRIKES ME as strange, as I walk, cycle, or drive along the village lanes, and hear reed warblers singing from virtually every corner, is that I am not hearing another summer visitor; one intimately connected with this species. In the time I have lived here, I have never once heard a cuckoo: a sound so closely associated with the coming of spring it is marked by annual letters to *The Times* newspaper.

Just after May Day, when the cuckoo's call should have been echoing across every village green in England, I bump into a neighbour of ours, Mick. He has spent his whole life in the parish, and his keen interest in birds makes him an oracle on changes in our local birdlife. I ask him if there used to be cuckoos here. 'Cuckoos?' he replies incredulously. 'Cuckoos! They used to drive us mad with their calling!'

Yet Mick hasn't heard one in the village for a decade or more. 'I suppose they're down the road at that new nature reserve . . .' he suggests. Sadly they are not: in half a dozen visits to Shapwick Heath this spring, I have heard just one.

The fate of the cuckoo in Somerset has been mirrored across much of lowland England, although the species does appear to be holding its own in Scotland, where cuckoos lay their eggs in the nests of meadow pipits, rather than reed warblers. Why cuckoos have declined, and so precipitously, we are not entirely sure. There is clearly a problem on the bird's wintering grounds, just south of the Sahara, which are rapidly turning into desert as a result of global climate change, which means that wintering cuckoos have nothing to eat.

It may also be because of a drop in numbers, here in Britain, of the larger caterpillars the young cuckoo needs in order to survive. And as with other late migrants such as the turtle dove and spotted flycatcher, a shift forward in the start of spring may be putting these birds 'out of sync' with their food supply; and in the cuckoo's case, with the lifecycles of its hosts.

What is certain, though, is that if this decline

continues, the cuckoo will eventually lose its place as the quintessential sign of the coming of spring. I doubt very much if the children at our village school have ever seen or heard a cuckoo. If they are aware of it at all, they probably place it in the same category as the dragon, the phoenix and other mythical creatures. In another decade or so, when cuckoos may well have disappeared from the whole of southern Britain, what will they mean to us then, beyond a set of old rural stories and sayings, growing less and less relevant as each year passes?

❈

THE REED WARBLER'S close relative, the sedge warbler, can also be found in the parish, but in much smaller numbers than its cousin. If seen well, the two are easy to tell apart: the sedge warbler's plumage is streaked rather than plain, and it has a prominent pale eyestripe, giving it a rather dapper appearance.

When I hear a sedge warbler singing, I am always struck by how different he sounds from his cousin. In contrast with the dull, repetitive and rather monotonous reed warbler, the sedge warbler is a manic little thing, the notes tumbling out of his bill as if, in his eagerness to deliver the message, he is tripping over his own tongue.

Sedge warblers – at least those I come across in Somerset – often sing from a high and prominent perch, giving me the chance to see their extraordinary orange gape. Sometimes, a singing bird will get so carried away he will launch himself into the air, fluttering momentarily against the summer sky before parachuting back down to his perch. Why the sedge warbler should be so confident, while the reed warbler is so shy, I have no idea. But as the reed warbler chunters away deep inside the reeds, it almost seems as if he is tutting disapprovingly at his relative's exhibitionist tendencies.

Another big difference between the two species is the way each chooses to migrate. Watching a brood of juvenile reed warblers clambering tentatively around the reeds, I find it hard to believe they could fly much further than the next rhyne. Yet in three or four months' time they will head off, hopping across the English Channel to the Low Countries, before turning south-west across France and Iberia, and then on to north-west Africa. From there they will continue south, travelling by night in short hops, until they end up in West Africa.

In keeping with their more extrovert personality, when it comes to migration, sedge warblers adopt an all-or-nothing strategy. They make more or less the same journey as the reed warbler, but do so in one or two giant leaps rather than a series of short hops. A naturalist friend of mine memorably describes the contrasting strategies as 'trickle and bounce'.

To prepare for their marathon flight, sedge warblers must put on weight, and lots of it. As early as July they start feeding on reed aphids, an ephemeral but sometimes abundant source of food. They lay down fat deposits beneath their skin, which appear as thick, orange-yellow blotches on birds I have seen in the hand. Once they have reached a critical mass – having almost doubled their body weight to about an ounce – they set off, some flying the three thousand miles or so to their winter quarters in a single go, straight across the Mediterranean and Sahara Desert.

Once they have left our shores, it is another seven months before they return. But next April and May, as I cycle the lanes of the parish, I shall once again hear the excitable flourish of the sedge warbler, and the steady drone of the reed warbler, echoing from the watery rhynes. For me, the arrival of these two little miracles will be the final sign that winter is well and truly over. And once again, as I do every spring, I shall try to imagine an army of millions of these birds as they swarm northwards across Europe, arriving in communities from Galway in the west to the Urals in the east, and as far north as Varanger Fiord, on the edge of the Arctic. And here, to our village in Somerset.

❀

ON THE CORNER of Perry Road and Blackford Road, next to Mill Batch Farm, a tumbledown brick building stands next to a small, unassuming tree, covered with small, curled, lime-green leaves. As they unfurl they reveal their rounded shape, coming to a shallow point at the tip, with a downy texture on the underside. For those of us who grew up before the 1970s, the shape and feel of these leaves is strangely familiar.

For this is the tree of my childhood: an elm. A row of elms used to back onto the garden of the house where I was brought up, creating a visual and aural barrier between us and the increasingly busy lane behind. But a few years later they began to wither and die, and were chopped down before they fell of their own accord. They were the victims of a scourge which all but removed this famous tree from the landscape of lowland Britain: Dutch elm disease.

Sadly the elm by Mill Batch Farm, despite its currently healthy appearance, will never grow into the magnificent, full-sized tree I can still recall. In a few years' time, a small beetle will invade the growing bark, and slowly but surely kill off its future. The same story is repeated throughout Britain, where the elm has become a 'ghost tree', present only in the form of these young saplings whose future is doomed. It is as if a whole generation of children has been blighted with some terrible inherited disease, which will never allow them to reach adulthood.

The reason for the elm's universal susceptibility to Dutch elm disease lies in its reproductive method. The English elm does not spread itself by seeds dispersing on the air, but by using suckers. This may be a highly efficient method, but it creates an Achilles heel: genetically, the trees are virtually identical, which means they are unable to develop resistance to the foreign invader.

Elms were never celebrated as much as the oak, but they were always a part of village life, growing along lanes and field boundaries throughout the country. When they disappeared, it was as if the heart had been torn out of the British countryside. Today the full-grown elm survives mainly in the works of landscape artist Rowland Hilder, which my mother used to hang above the mantelpiece: majestic avenues of tall trees, disappearing into the autumn mist.

❀

BY MID-MAY, THE broad hedgerows along the back lanes are in full flush. Unlike those few hedges that remain on the plains of East Anglia, or the high banks down the road in Devon, these are low, broad and solid – often wider than they are high.

They are created from a range of woody and thorny plants, including hawthorn, blackthorn, bramble and dog rose, and together they form a dense and impenetrable barrier dividing the fields, or between fields and lanes. Along with the rhynes and droves, they are the most typical feature of the parish landscape, and also one that is vitally important for wildlife.

For a few weeks at this time of year, the hedgerows are lined with a narrow strip of white: cow parsley, also known, rather more poetically, as Queen Anne's lace. This is surely the most familiar plant of rural Britain; there can hardly be a lane, road, or carriageway in the countryside where these tall, rangy plants cannot be seen during May and June.

In his delightfully quirky botanical history, *An Englishman's Flora*, Geoffrey Grigson lists more than fifty different local names for this familiar plant, many of which refer to its use as a food for livestock, including sheep as well as cows. Others, such as 'devil's parsley', are more sinister, and are probably a result of confusing this plant with its similar but deadly poisonous relative, hemlock.

Take a closer look at cow parsley, and in the centre of each tightly packed cluster of tiny white flowers you will see half a dozen or more tiny flies, which will help to pollinate the plant and continue its domination of our country lanes. But in the past few years, the cow parsley has had to compete with a brash, colourful newcomer. Tall green stems, each topped with a cluster of vivid yellow flowers, have sprung up everywhere. In some of the village lanes they threaten to overwhelm the incumbent plants, so complete is their dominance.

They have an unfair advantage; for this is no native hedgerow flower, but oil-seed rape. It is the product of agricultural policies that for many years have subsidised food production, with little or no thought for the consequences to the wider countryside and its wildlife. Agricultural plants have always escaped their field boundaries and cropped up elsewhere, and odd stems of wheat, barley and oats are a common sight throughout Britain. But there is something more sinister about rape: for true to its name, it doesn't just mix with the native wildflowers, but overwhelms them. The vibrant colour draws attention to itself like a footballer's wife in the royal enclosure at Ascot: the yellow is somehow unnatural, its electric brightness making it look as if it were created in a laboratory rather than in a field.

Rape has a long history as a cultivated plant. A member of the Brassica family, which includes cabbages, cauliflowers and turnips, it was grown for its oil in civilisations around the Mediterranean at least 3,000 years ago. It probably came to Britain with Bronze Age settlers; if not, the Romans certainly brought it here as a fuel for lighting. Having fallen out of fashion when we began to exploit fossil fuels, rape staged a major comeback in the latter part of the twentieth century, as a source of animal feed. Soon afterwards, those characteristic patches of bright yellow began to appear all over our countryside. It is still relatively scarce in these parts, where arable crops are rarely grown; but there is enough to produce these feral escapees, which dominate our waysides for a few weeks each May.

❊

FROM ONE RAMPAGING alien plant, to a sadly declining native bird: the nightingale. The nightingale is a paradox.

No other British bird has been so celebrated in verse and folklore, yet is so seldom seen. No other bird has such an extraordinary song, yet is so dull in appearance. And no other bird captures our imagination quite like this small, brown relative of the robin. Which given how scarce and elusive it is, might at first seem rather odd; until, that is, you witness the nightingale's performance for yourself.

Since moving to Somerset I have not had that pleasure, so on a fine May evening I decide to put things right. I head a few miles south of the parish, to the RSPB's West Sedgemoor reserve. Before the main event, I take a brief stroll, and finally catch up with another elusive bird: the cuckoo. For a few minutes, as the sun sets, I enjoy the spectacle of a trio of cuckoos, with one male chasing a female from bush to bush, as another calls in the distance.

By now I am ready to hear the solo performance of the nightingale. The song arrives out of nowhere, just as I am wandering back towards the car park, alongside a dense row of hawthorns. Two or three notes are all it takes for me to realise the identity of the songster. After tuning up, he delivers the full version: an unstoppable flood of deep, rich tones, interspersed with bizarre, mechanical sounds, which blend together to create this unique and unmistakable song.

Many have tried to describe the song of the nightingale; few have succeeded. But the novelist H. E. Bates certainly comes close:

It has some kind of electric, suspended quality that has a far deeper beauty than the most passionate of its sweetness. It is a performance made up, very often, more of silence than of utterance . . .

'More of silence than of utterance . . .' – the Harold Pinter of the bird world, perhaps. The popular songwriter Eric Maschwitz also celebrated the bird in the lyrics of his famous wartime song 'A Nightingale Sang in Berkeley Square'. And it is impossible to ignore the best-known poem about this species – perhaps about any British bird – John Keats's famous 'Ode to a Nightingale'.

But what about the subject of all this poetic attention – what exactly is a nightingale? The answer is something of an anticlimax. For the nightingale is just one of more than two hundred members of a family which includes the familiar robin, and various kinds of chats and flycatchers. Unlike its more colourful relations, such as the redstart, wheatear and bluethroat, it is essentially dull rufous-brown above, and paler beneath, with a reddish tinge to its tail.

So there can be little doubt that it is the nightingale's song, and especially its habit of singing through the night, which marks it out from its fellow songsters. Other birds also sing after dark – nocturnal robins often compete with nightingales – but nightingales do so with a persistence which makes their rivals appear half-hearted.

This may have something to do with the very brief period during which they sing; just a few weeks, from their arrival in April until the middle of June, when they fall silent. To make the most of this crucial time, nightingales have evolved the ability to sing throughout the night in a kind of 'arms race' between rival males. The birds with the most complex and persistent song are the most successful at attracting a mate, and so pass on their musical ability and singing stamina to future generations.

Sadly, this is a sound heard less and less often, both here and in the rest of Britain. We might expect a bird like the nightingale, on the north-western edge of its European range, to be doing rather well as a result of climate change. But in fact the species is in decline here, partly because of the destruction of its dense, scrubby habitat by an introduced, alien species, the muntjac deer.

Like the cuckoos I saw earlier, and other declining migrants such as the turtle dove and spotted flycatcher, the nightingale may also be suffering the consequences of changes in weather patterns in West Africa, where it spends the winter. Whatever the reasons, nightingale numbers have dropped by more than 90 per cent in my lifetime.

Despite their decline, nightingales can still be heard on fine spring evenings south and east of a line from the Severn to the Humber. It is an experience well worth having – for no amount of reading about this bird and its extraordinary song can prepare you for actually hearing it.

As I stand in the gloaming of a May evening, deep in the heart of rural Somerset, listening to the nightingale's song, I recall lines written by John Clare, almost two hundred years ago:

> *And still unseen, sings sweet – the ploughman feels*
> *The thrilling music, as he goes along,*
> *And imitates and listens – while the fields*
> *Lose all their paths in dusk, to lead him wrong*
> *Still sings the nightingale her sweet melodious song.*

For a few moments, I am able to immerse myself in this most complex and extraordinary sound. Then I walk back to the car park, and take the short drive home, the bird's sweet, melodious song still echoing in my mind.

❀

I RETURN HOME from work one evening to find a surprise in store: a jam jar containing a sleek, bronzed reptile; a slow-worm. This particular individual was discovered by my father-in-law Mike, on his driveway in Wedmore, a few miles to the east. Fortunately he spotted it before he got into his car, otherwise the Mini's tyres might have turned the slow-worm into a flat worm.

The children are agog with excitement, each wanting to take a turn holding the creature. I am impressed that they do so without fear, though when the animal begins to move George decides he has had enough. Daisy and Charlie, though, grasp it firmly but tenderly, heeding my warnings not to grip too tight. For like other lizards the slow-worm will, as a last resort, jettison its tail in order to escape being caught and eaten by a predator.

Neither slow nor indeed worms, slow-worms are beautiful creatures, and this one is no exception: a burnished bronze in colour; its firm, smooth skin marked with stripes along the length of the body. The young – which look rather like baby eels – are burnished gold, with a darker stripe along their spine.

With such large and noticeable eyes, it is surprising that this creature is sometimes known as the 'blind worm'. 'Slow-worm' seems equally inappropriate, and it actually derives from the Old English meaning 'slay worm', and refers to the creature's liking for earthworms. The slow-worm's scientific name, *Anguis fragilis*, literally means 'fragile snake'. But when a slow-worm blinks it reveals its true identity: snakes do not have eyelids, lizards do. The 'fragile' element derives from the aforementioned ability to protect itself against predators by losing its tail.

Another noticeable thing about slow-worms is their extraordinary longevity. They can survive for up to thirty years, rivalling the Komodo dragon as the world's longest lived lizard. But unlike the mighty dragon, which can reach a length of 10 feet or more, slow-worms rarely grow longer than 18 inches.

They are the most common of Britain's six species of reptile, with more than three-quarters of a million of them slithering around our grassy banks, hedgerows and gardens, so we might expect to see slow-worms more often than we do. But with so many hungry predators around, from birds to domestic cats, it pays to keep a low profile.

After taking a final look at our slow-worm, we decide to release it in a sunny spot next to our greenhouse, where long grass and brambles should provide protection and sanctuary. Like the field voles we trapped and released here a few weeks ago, it melts rapidly into cover, and away from our sight.

❦

ON A CLEAR day, looking due north of the village church, you can see the characteristic shape of Crook Peak. At almost 700 feet above sea level, this is one of the highest points on the Mendips, and the highest for some distance around. It is a well-known landmark, not least because it hoves into view as you head south along the M5 from Bristol to Exeter, marking the entrance to the county of Somerset. For me, it also marks the important dividing line between the West Country and the rest of Britain.

In our household, Crook Peak is always known as 'Charlie's mountain', the name given to it by our son when he first saw it from our garden a few summers ago. Now that he and the others are old enough, we regularly take a walk up to the top of the hill, to enjoy the view. We have climbed up here in the dead of winter, on a breezy autumn day, and in early spring, and it has always been windy.

But today, on a fine day towards the end of May, the wind has finally dropped, and we are able to enjoy the peak in uncharacteristically warm sunshine.

From the car park there are two main routes up Crook Peak: one a casual stroll along a muddy path through woods; the other a mad scramble up the steep scarp slope, followed by a swift hike up the main ridge. We choose the latter, and as soon as we begin our climb we are confronted with a profusion of late-spring butterflies.

There are common blues, fluttering from place to place on delicate sapphire wings; small heaths, bleached pale in the afternoon sun; and a single grizzled skipper, a tiny, grey-and-white butterfly easily mistaken for a day-flying moth. A movement catches my eye in the blue sky above: a male kestrel, hovering on stiff wings; and just behind, a pair of ravens tumbling through the air. I briefly get excited about a closer, bright red object; but this turns out to be a model glider.

We trudge onwards and upwards, as mountain bikers race past us down the slope. Reaching the rocky cairn at the top, we are rewarded by looking down on a magnificent landscape, only slightly marred by the motorway traffic snaking past beneath us. To the west, the Bristol Channel; to the south-west, Brent Knoll, the Polden and Quantock Hills; and further still, towards the horizon, the ridge of Exmoor, just visible through the heat-haze.

To the east, along the Mendip ridge, I can see Cheddar Gorge and, beneath it, Cheddar Reservoir gleaming in the sunshine. Further south, the church at Wedmore, and behind it the unmistakable outline of Glastonbury Tor. And immediately ahead of us, I can just make out the familiar shape of the church tower in my own parish, and the roof of our home; the first time I have seen it so clearly from here. A real-life geography lesson for the children.

Buoyed by the sight and the fine weather, we walk down the other side, accompanied by the clamour of stonechats, their call just like the sound of two pebbles being knocked together. Lower down, we pass through a scrubby wood where brimstone butterflies flutter in the glades: butter-yellow males, and a female, pale green below, so that when she closes her wings she resembles a fresh leaf. Eventually we emerge onto the lane, and walk past banks covered with bird's-foot trefoil back to the car park, where a welcome drink of lukewarm water awaits us. I wonder, briefly, what Crook Peak must have been like when it snowed – a tobogganist's paradise, no doubt.

JUNE

THE ODD CHOICES made by birds, when they look for a place to nest, never fail to amaze me. As well as the blackbirds and blue tits in our workshop, we now have great tits in our mailbox. Well, not our mailbox, to be exact, but the one belonging to our neighbours Dawn and Marc, directly opposite our side gate.

I discover this when our postwoman, Val, knocks on the door. Val has covered this delivery route for over forty years, and it takes a lot to surprise her, but even she is, for once, lost for words. I gingerly lift the lid of the plywood box. Even before I have opened it, I can hear the hissing sound of the adult bird inside, incubating a clutch of eggs. Sure enough, as daylight illuminates the interior, I can see a beady black eye looking up at me.

'Great tits,' I pronounce, to Val's evident delight. The birds are incubating half a dozen tiny eggs, little pale ovals spotted with reddish-brown, each barely the size of my fingernail. Val carefully writes out a warning to anyone else who might have the temerity to deliver mail here, tapes it neatly to the side of the box, and continues with her round.

Close up, the nest is a wonderfully intricate concoction of moss and grass, the cup carefully lined with sheep's wool, collected from the next-door field. The incubating female really is a thing of beauty: the rich tones of her green-and-yellow plumage contrasting with her black head, snow-white cheeks and broad black stripe down the centre of her breast.

This choice of nesting place might seem unusual to us, but from a bird's point of view, the mailbox is the ideal location. It provides a roomy, wooden home, facing east (so avoiding the sun during the afternoon, when it is at its strongest), and a neat slit at the front, wide enough for the adults to gain entry, but too narrow for a predator.

A week or so later I check the box again, and to my delight five tiny beaks immediately point skywards, begging instinctively for food. The chicks can hardly be more than a day or two old. Now, for the parents, the real hard work begins. Every single day for the next couple of weeks, they must bring back up to a thousand moth caterpillars, to satisfy their hungry brood. So during every hour of daylight they must each find more than thirty caterpillars: roughly one every two minutes. It is an astonishing statistic; even more so when you consider that the adult birds also need to feed themselves. No wonder they look so tatty and exhausted by the time the chicks eventually fledge and leave the nest.

By now, in early June, the breeding season is in full swing, not just here in the parish but throughout the country. The birds in the mailbox are just one of a couple of million pairs of great tits breeding in Britain. Each pair lays between seven and nine eggs, and some have a second brood, so upwards of twenty million eggs are laid each year, producing between ten and fifteen million fledged youngsters. That's an awful lot of caterpillars – more than a billion in all – just for this one species.

Considering that there are around 120 million pairs, of well over 200 different species of bird, breeding in Britain, each of which needs to feed one or more broods of young, the sheer scale of this annual event is astonishing.

In this parish alone there are thousands of pairs of breeding birds, of at least fifty different species; all the more reason why each of us should safeguard our own little corner of the countryside.

❀

A SPELL OF warm, sunny weather early this month means that along the lanes, every hedgerow, bush and tree looks as if it is about to burst; and as I stare intently at one hawthorn I can almost see the foliage growing outwards by the minute. Surely, if this fine weather continues, the trunks, branches and twigs will be unable to contain the green force within, and will simply explode.

On a warm, muggy evening, the volcano-like silhouette of Brent Knoll is bathed in yellow sunshine as it pokes through horizontal fingers of cloud. Opposite, towards Glastonbury Tor, a thick layer of grey fills half the sky, its folds and pleats as untidy as a teenager's duvet. A broad, squat section of rainbow is just visible in the gap between the cloud base and the distant Mendip Hills, its layered bands of colour illuminating the sky.

All around the village, thrushes and blackbirds continue to sing their evening song. Do they never tire of hearing those same notes and phrases, repeated hour after hour, day after day, during the breeding season? I do another quick calculation: if a thrush sings twenty distinct phrases a minute, for six or seven hours a day (and many carry on for far longer), then during the four months of the breeding season it will have sung close to 1 million times. I do hope the females are impressed.

As I pass along Vole Road, a crescendo of sound alerts me to a newly fledged brood of reed warblers. For almost two months, their parents have skulked in the depths of the reedbeds, but now these birds show the bravado of youth, as they clamber to the tops of the hedgerows and scold me for my presence. They test out their wings, flitting clumsily from twig to twig, and showing off their neat new juvenile plumage, warm rufous above and ochre-yellow below. I can hear the adult male chuntering away, blithely ignored by his offspring.

The recent fine weather has been welcomed by the village farmers, who are working late into the evenings to gather in the grass before the rain returns. The fields have been sheared as close as the local sheep, leaving a cropped yellowish surface in place of the former lush, deep green. In the past few decades there has been a noticeable shift from growing hay – which needs days of fine weather at just the right time of year – to silage, a more dependable crop, but one that lacks the romance of the old ways of haymaking. Across most of Britain the traditional hay meadow our grandparents would have known, with its annual extravaganza of wild flowers, is now just a fading memory.

For some creatures, however, it doesn't really matter which method is being used. Now that the tractor has passed, rooks and jackdaws throng the short turf, their sharp, pointed bills digging into the soil for leatherjackets to feed themselves and their youngsters, if any remain in the nest. Low across each newly cut field, swallows are vacuuming up flying insects disturbed by the mower's blades. In between those cut for silage, the other fields alongside the road retain a luxurious growth of summer vegetation: ribwort plantain, grasses and buttercups, intermingled with spikes of common sorrel, their nut-brown foliage showing up against the light green vegetation around them.

Along the rhynes and ditches, the surface of the water is completely covered with a thin film of duckweed; while the reeds themselves, although not quite as high as an elephant's eye, are certainly higher than mine. These waterways have at last got their own splash of colour, with tall, yellow flag irises – known locally as 'butter-and-eggs' – whose rich hue stands out from the duller greens and browns of the surrounding landscape. Described by the Victorian naturalist Richard Jeffries as 'bright lamps of gold', these stately plants brighten up even a dull June day.

Like every corner of the parish, Vole Road has its own special character. Here, the hedgerows are thicker, denser and closer together than the more open southern and eastern parts; and the landscape feels somehow more warm, snug and safe. Pheasants certainly think so: this is one of the few places where I regularly hear their distinctive, rough bark, and occasionally catch a glimpse of a cock bird strutting in the shadows of a tall hedgerow.

Pheasants have been in Britain for at least a thousand years, since the Norman Conquest, and it is thought they probably arrived even earlier, with the Romans. Originally from south-west Asia, they owe their ubiquity to being plump, easy to catch and good to eat: in some ways a fatal combination, yet also their trump card, for without their status as a game bird there would be far fewer. But in our parish, pheasants remain pretty thin on the ground. The land here is simply too wet for them to thrive, so there is little or no shooting; and without pheasant shooting there are usually very few pheasants. Certainly compared to the countryside in East Anglia they are quite a rarity here.

The biggest danger to the few resident pheasants comes from a supremely wily and adaptable local predator: the fox. And sure enough, as I head off northwards, I come across not just one, but two foxes, each standing alone in the centre of a large, open, recently mown field.

In recent years, as foxes have moved into our city centres, there has been much debate about the habits of this opportunistic mammal. Several observers have concluded that urban foxes are more or less the same as their rural cousins. Genetically this may be true, but behaviourally they are worlds apart. Having lived in both city and countryside, I know that if I so much as look at a rural fox, it will turn and run; whereas their urban cousins will stare you down with an expression bordering on insolence. In this part of rural England at least, foxes know to fear any man; even though I carry no weapon, and mean them no harm.

As the sun finally sets over Brent Knoll, the sky to the east is awash with rain, and the grey blanket is drifting rapidly eastwards, chasing the departing light. Jackdaws head west towards the church tower, chacking away into the gloom. And as night finally falls, and the villagers settle down to watch the ten o'clock news, first pinpricks, then splashes, and finally great sheets of rain begin to fall.

❀

THE RAIN IS, as always, welcomed by the village gardeners, whose lawns and flower beds are beginning to suffer from this long, dry spell. And welcomed, too, by the local farmers, including our neighbour Rick. I say neighbour, but although Rick owns the farmyard next door, he actually lives several miles away on the western side of the village. Like many farmers in these parts, he owns scattered parcels of land all over the parish and beyond, including the wet meadows of Tealham Moor.

Back in April, I bumped into Rick at the Highbridge Young Farmers' seventy-fifth anniversary dinner and dance. As neither of us is known for his ballroom skills, we got talking about local customs, so many of which are dying out. He told me that before the war his late father Reg, something of a local legend, used to go bat-fowling.

To Rick's surprise, I knew what he meant by this peculiar phrase. Also known as bird-batting, it involved using a torch to flush roosting birds, then catching them in a large net. Apparently Reg and his friends wandered along the village's hedgerows on autumn nights, catching thrushes and blackbirds. 'What happened to them?' I asked innocently. 'He ate them,' Rick replied with commendable brevity.

Rick then tried out another local custom on me: ray-balling. This time, I had no idea what he meant, so he explained that it is a way of luring eels in order to catch them. And when he told me that he still goes out ray-balling on summer evenings, I asked if I might tag along.

❀

THE INVITATION COMES out of the blue, on the evening after the heavy rains. Children are fed, my weekly badminton game cancelled, and as dusk falls we head eastwards to Tealham Moor, filled with a delicious anticipation. We are a mixed bunch: Rick, his wife Heather, various sons, daughters-in-law and friends, and our leader Dennis. Large and bearded, with a ready wit, strong opinions and a jaw that gets plenty of exercise, Dennis is definitely a local character. Now in his sixties, he has been ray-balling for more than half a century, ever since his grandfather first took him out on a warm summer's night, back in the 1950s.

With ray-balling, as with many country pursuits, the equation between effort and reward might seem tipped against it. The work required to assemble the equipment, all of which needs to be made at home, seems colossal. But as Dennis explains, with an eel providing more protein than a fillet steak, it is well worth it.

For an hour before sunset, in Rick's farmyard, Dennis and Rick have threaded dozens of worms (collected by the bucketful the previous night) onto strong, stout pieces of thread. The worms form a series of concentric rings, which when dipped into the water fan out into a sphere: the ray-ball itself.

On the lower, northern bank of the Brue, next to a Second World War pillbox, Dennis finds the perfect spot. As dusk falls, we sit on the soft, yielding riverbank, and dip our metal poles into the murky water. Midges bite, bats flit in the star-studded darkness and, somewhere in the distance, a pheasant coughs twice, before falling silent.

Ray-balling is, Dennis tells me, a contact sport. Along the length of the pole I can feel the muddy bottom of the river and, following his advice, I slowly move the pole up and down, allowing the scent of the worms to disperse through the water. Eels hunt by smell, swimming upstream and eating everything they can find. Once they have grabbed onto something with their powerful jaws, it takes a lot to make them let go; a strength we hope to turn into a weakness, allowing us to catch them.

Time passes without a single bite, as the metallic calls of a nearby moorhen echo in the darkness. Then, without warning, I feel a tug on the pole, and a vibration. I lift it out of the water, but too tentatively, seeing a silvery flash disappear back into the river. I may have had first bite, but am annoyed that I let it go. 'Now you can see why I call it a contact sport,' laughs Dennis.

Twenty minutes later, another tug, another vibration. This time I lift the pole in one rapid sweep, and somehow manage to get it over the metal tub Dennis has placed in the river. I have judged it right: and a long, yellowish-green creature drops off the bunch of worms and into the tub. An eel: not a very big one, but an eel nonetheless.

Of all the creatures I have seen in the parish, the eel must surely have the most extraordinary life cycle. All the world's baby eels – known as elvers – are born in the depths of the Sargasso Sea, in the Atlantic Ocean between the West Indies and Bermuda. Once hatched, these tiny fish drift across the ocean, carried by the warming currents of the Gulf Stream until, several years later, they reach the waters around Britain. Gradually, the tide washes them into our estuaries, including Bridgwater Bay to the west of here. Then they travel inland: some swimming upstream, others, incredibly, wriggling over the land. Once they are in the river system they feed and grow for many years. Finally, having reached maturity, they head back to the

Sargasso Sea, a journey of some three thousand miles, where they lay their eggs and die.

Once eels were so common in these parts that, according to the Domesday Book, they were used to pay the rent. Even in my lifetime, villagers recall seeing hundreds of eels thrashing around in farm pools during thundery weather, desperate for oxygen; or watching them cross over the land, slithering over muddy fields on their way from one watercourse to another.

But in the past twenty years, the numbers of elvers coming upstream has plummeted. No one knows exactly why: it could be that climate change has caused a shift in the ocean currents; or perhaps barriers installed to control flooding are blocking their way. One sure reason for the decline is the illegal poaching of elvers, which are caught in their tens of thousands, and sold as a delicacy to the Asian market at more than £200 a pound. So eels are no longer the abundant creature they once were; and if the decline continues, they may soon disappear from our rivers.

Dennis tells us stories of the old days, when half a dozen people would gather along this very stretch of riverbank, catching eel after eel; sometimes well over a hundredweight in a single night. He would take them home, skin them and soak them overnight in brine, and in the morning fry them up with butcher's bacon: 'All fat – not a bit of lean!' The neighbours enjoyed the bounty too: Dennis would give away half the eels, and feast on the rest for days afterwards. As he speaks, that balance between effort and reward makes perfect sense.

Though not, sadly, this time. At one in the morning, we call it a night. The eel I caught is still the only one in the tub: a slender, pale creature, perhaps one foot long, and weighing 4 or 5 ounces. Nevertheless, it has been a privilege to take part in this ancient rural custom, and to hear how it was once part and parcel of seasonal life here on the levels. And as Dennis sagely notes, 'Fishing isn't about catching. If it were about catching, it'd be called "catching", not "fishing".'

We let the eel go, and it slithers away into the murky waters, out of sight.

❦

OTHER CREATURES OF the night are less elusive, though just as enigmatic as the eel. There are roughly 2,500 different kinds of moths in Britain, compared with fewer than 60 species of butterfly. Yet although they are here in their millions, during the long summer days they are virtually invisible. Our lives only occasionally intersect, when coincidences in time and space collude to bring us together.

On warm summer nights, as I drive home after dark, I see them reflected in my headlights as they flutter around the back lanes of the parish. Early in the mornings, my daughter Daisy brings me one clasped in her hands, caught as it tried to escape through the bathroom window. And on hot summer Sunday afternoons as I push the lawnmower over the lush grass, they shoot out from beneath its blades, temporarily evicted from their home.

To enter the mysterious world of moths, and reveal their bizarre beauty, we must resort to trickery. So at dusk, on a warm, overcast June evening, I set the trap. This is a large, circular, black plastic tub, with a round hole at the centre of its lid, onto which a mercury vapour bulb is mounted. When illuminated, this acts like a magnet for every moth in the area, drawing them inexorably in to investigate this unexpected source of light.

The theory behind the trap is a simple one. Moths use the moon to navigate, so when they encounter this incredibly bright light, they use it to orient themselves. But because the light is only a few yards away – compared with roughly 250,000 miles from my garden to the moon – they fly around it in rapidly decreasing circles, until they reach the centre of the trap.

The bulb is bright but cool, so they avoid being fried as they come into contact with its surface. After bumping into it they drop down, and slide effortlessly down plastic chutes into the tub, unable to escape. There is no need for food: most adult moths never feed anyway, as their caterpillars have done enough eating for one lifetime. So they simply hide away among the egg cartons I have placed there for that very purpose, and wait until morning.

As I turn the light on, and watch as its dull, purplish

glow begins to strengthen, I am immediately aware of the presence of moths. The ubiquitous large yellow under-wings bash into me as they fly headlong towards the trap. A buff ermine – furry, creamy-yellow, with delicate strokes of black – lands momentarily on my leg, before it too launches itself in the direction of the light. And all over the lawn, tiny, wraith-like grass moths begin their nocturnal adventures.

Another, larger moth is fluttering over the lawn, ignoring the attractions of the trap. Like a helicopter hovering above a rainforest, it moves steadily up and down across the same patch of grass, in a rhythmic, purposeful movement. It is a ghost swift, and of all our moths I think it the most bewitching. This is a male: an inch long and pure white in colour. In the twilight the whiteness makes him look larger than he is; his wings fluttering in an incessant blur, creating a haunting image on my retina.

His behaviour may appear odd, but he is doing it for a reason. The female, larger and yellower than the male, is hiding somewhere in the long grass below, giving off a pheromone that drives the male into this frenzied state. So as darkness falls, he swings to and fro like a pendulum, desperately seeking her out, until eventually she puts him out of his misery by reaching up to pull him down into her grassy lair to mate.

But as I watch the ghost swift swing to and fro over the lawn, its nocturnal perambulations equal in beauty and complexity to any of nature's courtship rituals, I forget about any scientific explanation for this bizarre behaviour, and simply enjoy the show.

✺

NEXT MORNING, THE ghost swift has vanished, but the trap is filled with a profusion of his relatives. Opening a moth trap is the bug-hunters' equivalent of Christmas morning, except that all your presents are trying to escape. The trick is to catch as many of the interesting moths as possible, temporarily incarcerating them in small, plastic containers in order to get a good view; and, if possible, identify them. I am always struck by their sheer variety: from tiny 'micros', so small and obscure I don't even try to give them a name, to huge hawkmoths, the most prized members of this panoply of shape, form and colour.

The evocative names of these moths link us directly with the naturalists who chose them. Take the selection I have before me on this bright June morning: blood vein, mottled beauty, light emerald, white ermine, buff ermine, heart and dart, flame shoulder, common wainscot, poplar grey, angle shades, marbled minor, burnished brass, ruby tiger, riband wave and straw dot.

What wonderful, imaginative, utterly bizarre names. Names bestowed by eccentric Victorian naturalists, who sought out their quarry with net, lamp and chloroform, pinning them to a board, then hiding them away in polished oak cabinets for later generations to open in wonder. Names I now hear on my children's lips, as they gleefully point out a familiar visitor, or question me about the identity of a new one.

Just like birds, some of these moths are residents, living the whole of their brief lives within the borders of the parish. Others, like the silver Y, are migrants, flying here all the way from Spain each summer. The silver Y is named after the distinctive Y-shaped marking on its wings; also reflected in its scientific name, *Autographa gamma*.

One of the objects in the trap doesn't, at first sight, resemble a living creature at all. Just over an inch long, silvery-grey in colour, it looks exactly like the twig of a silver birch; roughly snapped off at one end and neatly cut with a sharp penknife at the other, to reveal clean, bright, yellowish-buff wood.

Then this inanimate object does something dazzling. It opens its wings, revealing that it isn't a twig at all, but a moth: the buff-tip. The buff-tip is one of the most remarkable creatures I am ever likely to see in my garden. Not because it is rare – there are three in the trap this morning – but because it is the finest example I have ever seen of animal camouflage. The shades and markings exactly mimic a birch twig, even down to the rough silvery film on the surface. When it closes its wings, only two antennae, poking unobtrusively out of the narrow end, reveal that it is alive at all. It makes the chameleon look like a rank amateur.

The other extraordinary moth in this morning's

selection sports one of the loveliest combinations of colour I have ever seen in nature, or indeed anywhere else. About 1½ inches long and 2 inches across, its body and wings are a deep olive-green with a yellowish tinge, streaked with a lurid salmon-pink, as if it has been coloured with a fluorescent highlighter pen. If this combination of colour and design appeared on the Paris catwalk, you wouldn't be at all surprised.

It is an elephant hawkmoth, so named not because it resembles an elephant, which it doesn't, but because its larva does. About 3 inches long, the caterpillar sports a proboscis like an elephant's trunk, which it waves at its enemies to confuse and frighten them. Sadly these, and other large and noticeable hawkmoth caterpillars, are often killed by fearful householders, who remain ignorant of the beauty that lies within, ready to emerge once the creature has pupated.

I allow this stunning vision to crawl onto my hand, where it pauses for a moment, before heading off low across the garden on whirring wings. It is seeking out a clump of fuchsias, where it will hang for the rest of the day, its gaudy colours the perfect camouflage against this flamboyant flower. Then, along with the hundred or so moths I have released, and the many millions I failed to catch, it will emerge at dusk, to patrol the lanes, gardens and flower beds of the parish until dawn breaks once again.

❁

MOST YEARS, SOMETIME between late April and the middle of June, the weather systems above the British Isles shuffle around the skies to create the pattern we are all hoping for: a building ridge of high pressure, bringing southerly breezes, warm air and clear skies.

In the early afternoons, the temperatures push into the low 20s, though with cloudless skies at night it can still be quite chilly at dawn. In the evenings, though, a residue of the day's heat still remains. So as the evening star, the planet Venus, rises in the darkening sky over Mill Batch Farm, there is just enough warmth to bring the moths out to feed, and with them, their predators: pipistrelle bats.

Our smallest bat, and by weight our smallest mammal, the pipistrelle is a wonder. Barely the length of my thumb-joint, and weighing less than a sixth of an ounce – about the same as a two-pence coin – this is the bat we usually catch a glimpse of on spring and summer evenings, fluttering in the gloaming as it hunts down flying insects. Found throughout the UK, it can be seen in suburbs, towns and gardens, as well as rural areas such as our parish.

Pipistrelles are something of a paradox: they are common, and yet, like all our bat species, can be very hard to see. In early spring, about two million individuals emerge from their winter hibernation in trees and buildings, to flutter across our evening skies. But sadly, there aren't as many as there used to be. Just as many insect-eating birds have declined in the past few decades, so these tiny bats have also seen a fall in numbers. It's the old, familiar story:

a combination of the overuse of agricultural chemicals, habitat loss and, just like garden birds, the hunting skills of that ubiquitous but alien creature, the domestic cat.

The pipistrelle may be familiar, but this modest, often overlooked little animal has an amazing story to tell. Its secret – perhaps I should say *their* secret – was revealed a few years ago, thanks to Britain's growing army of bat watchers.

Bats locate their prey in darkness by using a technique called 'echolocation': emitting a series of high-pitched sounds, mostly too high for our ears to hear, which 'bounce off' flying objects such as moths, and enable the bat to home in on its quarry. So we need to use handy little machines called bat detectors, which can transform these inaudible sounds into a series of clicks we are then able to hear. By adjusting a dial on the detector, we can read the frequency of an individual bat, and thus attempt to assign it to a particular species.

I venture outside at dusk, a permanent shushing sound emanating from the little box of knobs and dials I am carrying. Conveniently, the bat detector has a luminous screen and digital display, with a scale ranging from 16 to 120 kilohertz. So far, however, I have failed to detect anything at all. This is partly due to my inexperience with the device, and partly because to use it successfully, I have to guess which bat I might be 'hearing', and set the dial accordingly.

To my inexpert eyes, it looks like a good evening for

bats. An hour ago, the sun finally set over the farmyard, and the last swallows dropped down into the barn to seek refuge for the night. In the gloaming I can just make out a thick deposit of soft manure, left by the cattle. This is, I hope, attracting hordes of invisible flying insects: bat food.

And then I see my first bat, fluttering and swerving in the paler sky above the gable end of the barn. It swoops down, past the telegraph wires where the swallows sit by day, whizzes past my head, through the narrow gap between the young elm trees, and out of the yard. To me this looks like a miracle, but for an echolocating bat it is all in a night's work.

So which species is it? It is small, which means it's most likely to be a common pipistrelle. I set the dial to 45 kilohertz – the frequency at which this particular bat normally echolocates – but the device fails to respond. Have I not turned up the volume? Is there a connector missing? I turn the dial backwards and forwards, but still nothing. Meanwhile the bat is obviously hunting, and catching, moths, and presumably using echolocation to do so. Then I have a flash of inspiration. I carefully turn the dial up the scale ... 46 ... 48 ... 50 ... 52 ... 53 ... 54 ... 55 ... and bingo! Clear as day, through the magic machine, I hear a series of rapid, rhythmic clicks, a dozen or so in all.

I have just re-enacted one of the most extraordinary events in British natural history: the discovery of the soprano pipistrelle. Back in the last year of the old millennium, bat experts noticed something unusual when they were observing pipistrelles. Some of the bats they 'heard' with their detectors were echolocating at 45 kilohertz, but others were doing so at a higher frequency: 55 kilohertz.

When they took a closer look at the behaviour of both groups of bats, they discovered, to their astonishment, that these led separate lives, with slightly different food and habitat needs. This was enough to formally 'split' one pipistrelle species into two new ones: the common pipistrelle and the soprano pipistrelle.

This may sound like something only of interest to bat enthusiasts, but nothing could be further from the truth. The discovery of what is known as a 'cryptic species' brings the tantalising possibility that there might be dozens more of these hidden creatures out there. Could there possibly be two different species of house sparrows, blue tits, foxes, or rabbits, living alongside each other, undetected by us, but definitely leading separate lives? The discovery revealed just how little we know about some of the wild creatures we take for granted and how much more there might be to discover. In a nation where we pride ourselves on knowing almost everything about our native wildlife, this is an exciting, and rather humbling, thought.

Delighted to have discovered this creature for myself, I watch as the soprano pipistrelle performs like the opera singer after whom it is named. It flies around my head, clicking as it goes, swerving in figures of eight through the sky, and grabbing unsuspecting moths out of the darkness. And thanks to the miracle machine in my hand, I can momentarily enter its mysterious nocturnal world.

✵

THROUGHOUT THE YEAR, but especially in May and June, our dense hedgerows and reedbeds are home to a bird that most of the village's residents ignore, probably because it looks a bit like a house sparrow. Or rather the female does: though a closer look does reveal a rich, chestnut tone to her plumage, with greyer underparts, and fine streaks on her head and face. If you thought you might be looking at something different from a common or garden sparrow, a glimpse of the male would confirm your suspicions. For the male reed bunting is a splendid-looking bird, sporting a jet-black head and face, snow-white collar, and white 'moustaches' on either side of his bill.

Like so many farmland birds, reed buntings have suffered major declines during my lifetime, although a cycle ride around the lanes of the parish might make you think otherwise. Reed buntings are everywhere: in winter they gather in loose flocks, flitting among the thick hedgerows in search of food; and now, in summer, they have moved to the small patches of reeds along the rhynes. Here, from April to August, the males sing their curiously unassuming song, which always sounds to me rather like a bored sound engineer: 'one . . . two . . . one . . . two . . . testing . . . testing'.

But although reed buntings have made something of a comeback, the same cannot be said for three of their close relatives: the yellowhammer, corn and cirl buntings. All three species have declined in numbers and contracted in range since the Second World War, and although yellowhammers can still be found in the more arable parts of Somerset, corn buntings have disappeared from the county, with just a single record in the past couple of winters. If we wanted an emblem of what has gone wrong in the British countryside, we need look no further than the fate of the corn bunting: a bird our ancestors would have taken for granted, but which we have allowed to vanish from much of the rural scene.

The decline of the cirl bunting has been even more precipitous; indeed at one point it looked as if this attractive little seed-eater might go extinct as a British bird. When I was a boy the cirl bunting could be found widely, though locally, across southern England. But from the 1980s onwards its range retreated rapidly towards the south-west, so that today it is virtually confined to a narrow coastal strip of south Devon. There, thanks to the work of the RSPB and local farmers, its fortunes have finally turned a corner. This would have pleased one of my ornithological heroes, George Montagu, who two centuries ago first discovered cirl buntings in Britain, in the small, tightly hedged fields around his south Devon home.

Could the cirl bunting ever make a comeback, and return to breed here in Somerset? Left to its own devices, probably not: this is a stay-at-home bird, rarely travelling more than a mile or two in the whole of its lifetime. So it needs a helping hand. Given that they have already been successfully reintroduced into Cornwall, perhaps Somerset could be the next place to release them; en route to repopulating the rest of southern England with this modest but attractive little bird.

❀

By the middle of the month, the vegetation in the meadow at the bottom of our garden is reaching triffid-like proportions. On warm, sunny mornings, as rafts of cumulo-nimbus clouds rise into the bright blue sky, clumps of hogweed are awash with insects, large and small.

Hogweed is one of the great unsung heroes of the British summer. Taller than a grown man, its broad, flat, creamy-white flower-heads are supported on robust stalks as thick as my fingers. As the name suggests, hogweed was traditionally gathered as a supplementary food for farm livestock: local Somerset names include 'cowbelly', 'pig's parsnip' and my favourite, 'pig's bubble'. The hollow green stalks were also used as makeshift straws for drinking the local brew, cider. Today, as on any warm summer's day, smaller creatures are using the hogweed for drinking as well. Bluebottles, greenbottles and hoverflies all gather to feed on the supplies of nectar produced by these huge flower-heads, which viewed from the side look like fields of snow.

Among these run-of-the-mill insects is a rather splendid specimen: a green dock-leaf beetle. This is a pregnant female, its swollen abdomen a striking coppery colour, contrasting with its metallic-green head. The dock plant beneath the hogweed is covered with its tiny larvae, along with the much smaller and less distinctive male.

As a blackcap sings its fluty song in the apple tree above, a ladybird alights to join the throng. A closer look confirms my suspicions: this beautiful scarlet-and-black insect is larger, squatter and flatter than any of our native species. It is an alien invader: the harlequin ladybird. The bizarre thing about the harlequin is that it is so variable in appearance: some are pillar-box red, with fifteen or more black spots; others are jet-black with reddish-orange spots; and a few are pale orange, with virtually no visible spots.

Harlequin ladybirds were, until a few years ago, almost unknown in Britain. But in the past decade this colourful insect, originally from eastern Asia, has reached our shores. It almost certainly arrived on plants imported by garden centres and, in a frighteningly short time, it has become the default ladybird. Here in the parish, indeed in my own garden, they now seem to be more common than the native two-spot and seven-spot varieties; which, if the doomsayers are to be believed, may now be heading rapidly towards extinction, having been outcompeted by their larger relative.

Further down the garden, the mellifluous tones of the blackcap are replaced by a series of strident and persistent 'hoo-eet' sounds. These come from a pair of chiffchaffs, whose neat, olive-green spring plumage has faded to the shade of a milky cup of tea. Their tatty appearance bears witness to several weeks of effort finding food for their chicks, which have now left their nest, and are hidden away in the dense lime-green foliage of our cider-apple trees.

Here, in the sunniest, warmest part of the garden, among sunshine-yellow meadow buttercups and creeping buttercups, electric-blue matchsticks hover from plant to plant. These are common blue and azure damselflies, beautiful insects which can only be told apart by examining the pattern on the first two segments of their abdomen, immediately behind the thorax. Take a closer look, and you'll notice that the pattern on the common blue looks like an oak tree, while that on the azure damselfly bears a remarkable similarity to the Honda logo. Bizarre, but true.

People are often puzzled about the difference between damselflies and dragonflies. Size is a good guide: most dragonflies are fairly large, while damselflies are small, though there are a few exceptions. But the easiest way to tell them apart is when they perch: damselflies hold their wings tight to their body (or in a few cases, at a 45-degree angle), whereas dragonflies perch with their wings held at right angles to their body, recalling a First World War biplane.

As if on cue, a larger, yellowish-brown insect catches my eye as it zooms past. It is undoubtedly a dragonfly, but which one? It perches briefly on a head of hogweed, its squat upper abdomen tapering to a point at the tip. This, together with its colour and pattern, marks it out as the most common dragonfly of early summer, the four-spotted chaser.

This name is something of a misnomer, as each wing actually has two spots, making eight in all. The body is a melange of yellows, ochres and browns; but the most striking feature is the delicate yellow latticework along the forward edge of the front wings, known as the 'costa'. It is a beautiful insect to see, especially in my own garden. But what worries me – especially on such a fine, warm and sunny day – is the virtual absence of butterflies. Only the odd speckled wood and large white can be seen, despite an abundance of nectar for them to feed on.

Our garden has proved to be, over the years, something of a hotspot for butterflies, with no fewer than twenty species recorded here – one third of the British total. As well as the usual kinds, I've seen brown argus and marbled white, small copper and common blue, and the long-distance migrants, clouded yellow and painted lady. But three unusually wet summers in a row have taken their toll.

As I walk back towards the house, I realise that what

used to be a pristine lawn, mown within an inch of its life by the previous owners, has already passed through the stage of being a grassy meadow and, on the sunny, south-facing side, is rapidly reverting to scrub. Ash, elm and apple saplings, some well over my own height, compete with each other for diminishing space. If I don't do something – and fairly soon – in another few years the meadow will have turned into a full-scale copse.

❀

AT THIS TIME of year, the walls around the parish are suddenly ablaze with a striking flower, red valerian, whose colour and texture remind me of something out of a Laura Ashley catalogue. For a few weeks, from mid-June to mid-July, this attractive and conspicuous plant is thriving. It may be called red, but in truth the colour is a kind of deep pink: some plants shade towards the violet end of the spectrum, others have a more russet – and to my eye, more pleasing – tone. Occasionally, a striking snow-white variant appears among its neighbouring blooms.

Like so many of our wall-loving plants, red valerian is an immigrant, originally brought to Britain from the Mediterranean during Tudor times, to adorn rockeries in ornamental gardens. After a couple of hundred years it managed to escape from confinement, and has since spread across much of England and Wales, though its stronghold remains here in the West Country.

Given the visual dominance of these gaudy flowers, it would be easy to overlook some of the less ostentatious botanical residents of the village. Fortunately, given my lack of expertise on all things botanical, my friend and colleague Brett has agreed to accompany me on an evening's cycle ride around the back lanes of the parish, to open my eyes to the floral wonders I might otherwise miss.

In the old stone wall that runs alongside the road by the White Horse Inn, we come across ivy-leaved toadflax, flowering in profusion. Like the red valerian, this is also an import from abroad, having been brought here from southern Europe in the early seventeenth century. The delicate, tiny, lobed leaves are held by thin stalks, which support hundreds of exquisite flowers: pale lilac in shade, with custard-yellow centres. Its scientific name, *muralis*, indicates its preferred habitat. This plant propagates itself in a most ingenious way. Whereas the shoots of most plants grow towards the sun, those of the toadflax are 'helio-phobic', growing away from the light. So once flowering is over, the seed-heads bend downwards, burrowing into the cracks and crevices of the walls, and thus enabling the plant to find new places to grow.

Brett points out that the stone itself is not a natural feature of the local landscape, but was brought here from the nearby Mendips. The damp, shaded side of this wall is also covered in ferns, including the splendidly named maidenhair spleenwort. Its long, narrow stalks support pairs of pale, lime-green leaves; the overall effect, if you have a fairly vivid imagination, a little like a young girl's hair. A closer look reveals a smaller fern, a rusty-back; its leaves are encrusted with copper-coloured scales, the texture of soft felt.

The ditches along Vole Road are filling up with plant life too, much of it of the floating variety. Duckweed and frogbit, looking rather like a miniature water lily, dominate. But from time to time I come across mats of water violet, with its tiny, pale lilac-pink flowers, whose feathery foliage covers the surface so effectively it looks as if you could walk right across without getting your feet wet. Quite a scarce plant, it thrives in these parts, where it is called by a variety of local names, including 'cat's eyes' and 'featherfoil'. At the water's edge, I see the yellow flowers of celery-leaved buttercup, another fairly common plant in these muddy places. Its attractive yellow flowers conceal a rather unpleasant trait: the sap can poison cattle and cause human skin to break out in blisters: hence its alternative name of 'cursed crowfoot'.

The cow parsley and oil-seed rape that so dominated the byways of the parish a month or so ago have now died back. Their place has been taken by stands of hogweed which, as in my own garden, are covered with feeding insects. Nearby, on a metal five-barred gate, Brett spots another, larger insect. About half an inch long, it is a snipe-fly, often called the 'down-looker fly' because of its unusual habit of resting with its head pointing down towards the ground. The name snipe-fly is supposed to be due to its attenuated shape, like a snipe's bill. But I wonder if it might also be due to its mottled coloration; the reddish-brown abdomen resembling the plumage of a snipe.

The foliage along the ditches is home to what seem at first sight to be a whole range of different kinds of mollusc. Snails of all shades and patterns abound: some pale yellow, others strikingly black and white. Yet, in fact, all these snails belong to the same species, the white-lipped banded snail, also known as 'humbug snails' from their resemblance to the old-fashioned children's sweet. Despite their varied appearance, these snails are genetically almost identical to each other – a bit like us, really.

❦

ON MIDSUMMER'S EVE, the half-moon rises in the southern sky. From the ancient drove that runs eastwards between Kingsway and Perry Road I can see, as usual, the church tower to the south, with the silhouette of Crook Peak to the north.

An upturned, rusting bathtub, once a drinking trough for the local cattle, marks the halfway point along the drove. The hedgerows are taller and thicker than else-where in the parish; and are cut less frequently, creating high barriers on either side of the path. From deep within, a whitethroat utters its scolding call. The cowpats are hard as nails, as is the ground; very different from the muddy sludge I tramped through last winter.

I am stirred from my reverie, first by a male pheasant shooting up from just beneath my feet; then by two roe-bucks which appear where the drove narrows, just before it emerges onto the lane. The first leaps out right in front of me, pauses, and looks round momentarily, before stotting away like an antelope on the African savannah. He is swiftly followed by the other, and for a moment I am able to take in the beauty of this, the smaller of our two native deer species. Each sports a tan coat, shading darker along the back; a quizzical face, framing a round, black nose, and long, pricked ears, with two short, pointed horns sticking straight up between them.

The two bucks leap along the path before veering sharply off to the right, and plunging straight through a narrow gap in the hedge. I cycle along to where they disappeared, and peer through; they are already on the other side of the newly mown field, at least 200 yards away. In the weakening sunlight their tan colour stands out against the dark green foliage, as they stare towards me, ever alert to danger.

Roe deer were hunted to extinction in England by the start of the eighteenth century, although they did manage to hang on in the wilder parts of Scotland. The Victorians brought them back here, and now I come across them in every season of the year: on cold days in winter, their breath freezing in the air; posing in the flower-covered fields in spring and summer; and in autumn, glowing in the late-afternoon sun. Yet any encounter with them – especially one as intimate as this one – always feels special.

As I reach the junction between the drove and the lane, I catch a glimpse of two more shy creatures: a pair of bullfinches, perched on the edge of a hawthorn bush. In a family renowned for its charm and beauty, the bullfinch still stands out. This is partly because of its appearance: few British songbirds are quite as stunning as the male, with his combination of black head, white rump and vibrant, cherry-pink breast. You might think he would show off his finery, but the bullfinch is a shy bird.

It is also, sadly, one of our most threatened, having declined dramatically throughout Britain during the past couple of decades, like so many other farmland and woodland birds. The bullfinch has never been popular where there are orchards, as it feeds on the young buds of fruit trees; enough to make enemies in this apple-growing county. But if you know where to look, bullfinches can still be found in the hedgerows and orchards of the parish. Often they reveal themselves by sound rather than sight: uttering their soft, plaintive, piping call, rather like a child's toy. It always strikes me as rather sad; but this is simply the way we impose our own, human emotions on wild birds. I'm sure to a female bullfinch it is the most beautiful sound in the world.

❀

As the fine, dry weather continues, the sound of the harvest being gathered in continues long into the evening. In the fields, in place of old-fashioned stooks of hay, there are now neat, round, glossy lumps of black polythene, like the droppings of a giant rabbit. Each casts a long evening shadow, its shiny surface reflecting a distorted image of the surrounding landscape. Their alien appearance in this rustic scene reminds me that whatever else we wish to use it for, the countryside remains primarily a food factory.

Perched on a hawthorn bush, facing into the evening sun, sits a family of linnets. The male still shows traces of the pink breast patches he sports during the breeding season; the female and the youngsters are brown, speckled greyish-buff beneath. The linnet is the forgotten bird of our pastoral landscape: neither as attractive as the yellow-hammer, nor as well known as the skylark. It is a quiet, modest creature, which like its relative the bullfinch has declined in the last few decades.

The linnet family flies off into the field, joining a larger flock of linnets and goldfinches. They flit among the meadow barley and Yorkshire fog, past meadow brown butterflies, while swallows hawk for insects a few feet above their heads. The linnets and goldfinches perch on the tops of sorrels and pick off the seeds, their weight hardly bending the stalks; then take off, bouncing into the air on long, delicate wings, and uttering their light, tinkling calls.

This is a welcome, though increasingly rare, sight. Fields in the parish, in the rest of Somerset and far beyond would once, at this time of year, have been filled with vast flocks of finches, buntings and sparrows. But the new agriculture – with productivity and efficiency at its core – has changed all this, by removing 'waste' seed that would have fed the birds.

In the hour before dusk, two small tortoiseshells sit on the dry path, trembling their wings to gain a tiny amount of extra energy so they can continue feeding. Close to, they look like sunbathing birds: the hairy head and thorax contrasting with the burnt-orange wings, marked along their edges with black and bluish-mauve spots.

Just like the linnet, the small tortoiseshell has become a far less frequent sight in recent years. This is since the arrival, spreading northwards, from continental Europe, of a new species of parasitic fly, *Sturmia bella*, which lays its eggs on the nettle leaves on which the tortoiseshell's caterpillars feed. Once the caterpillar has inadvertently digested the fly's eggs, the larva in turn devours the caterpillar from within. Having arrived on our shores a decade or so ago, this unwelcome parasite has rampaged throughout Britain, reducing small tortoiseshell numbers by half.

Who would have thought that within ten years the small tortoiseshell, rather like the house sparrow, would have become a creature we now notice because of its scarcity, rather than one we ignored because of its ubiquity?

❁

EVERY MORNING AND evening, during the village rush hour, if such a thing exists, our neighbours at Perry Farm drive their cattle the short stretch along the road to and from their pasture. The animals wander slowly towards the gate, by the sharp left-hand corner which marks the north-eastern border of our parish.

Every morning, and every evening, the cattle do what cattle do. And once the day's traffic has passed up and down, the cowpats are spread across the road like a thin layer of Marmite. Just before dusk falls, thousands of tiny insects gather to feed on the dung, while a brood of newly fledged pied wagtails comes to feed on the insects. They flutter back and forth on their new, inexperienced wings, taking advantage of this food bonanza.

Meanwhile, a pair of swans is sitting in the field just behind the small ditch by the entrance to Perry Farm. The male and female are guarding five small, fluffy cygnets – each well over a foot long – which hatched out only a few days ago. The original ugly ducklings sit, flanked by their proud parents, among piles of white, downy feathers. As I pass, on my cycle ride home, the male lowers his neck and hisses aggressively. I pray that he and his family pass a quiet night, with no visit from the local fox.

I realise, as I pedal the last short stretch back home, that half the year has gone.

JULY

JULY IS A month of stasis rather than dramatic change; a chance to reflect on the roller-coaster ride of the spring, and look ahead to the coming autumn. April was full of activity, as migrant birds arrived back in the parish from Africa, adding their voice to the resident chorus. Sunny days in May saw an onrush of wild flowers and butterflies; while on warm June nights huge and colourful hawkmoths, and dark and mysterious bats, emerged from their daytime hideaways.

Soon, in August, swifts will pass overhead, flying purposefully south; and by September the swallows will gather on the telegraph wires, as red admirals bask beneath our cider-apple trees, enjoying the last warm rays of sunshine. But for now the whole scene is dulled by the lazy heat of long summer days. Even the dawn chorus is over: the tuneful orchestra that woke us each morning replaced by the incessant chacking of jackdaws, the plaintive cries of our neighbour's peacocks, and a distant, mournful wood pigeon. There's a good reason for this lapse into near silence. Now that the hard work of raising a family is over, the parent birds are hidden away in thick foliage, moulting into a brand-new set of feathers, in preparation for the colder weather to come. The youngsters are lying low, too, keeping out of sight to avoid the attentions of the local cats and sparrowhawks.

My own attention has turned from birds to their smaller flying counterparts. July is the peak month for butterflies and moths, bumblebees and hoverflies, all making the most of abundant nectar in the hedgerows and flower beds around the village. As I make my way slowly along the wide and bumpy droves, I am accompanied by a constant hum; the sound of millions, perhaps billions, of insects, as they live out their brief lives among us in this quiet country parish.

❀

OF ALL THE insects that buzz, hum and flutter along the lanes, one of my favourites is the gatekeeper butterfly. Also known as the hedge brown, this alluring creature is a smaller and more elegant version of the widespread meadow brown butterfly. I am always struck by the brightness of the first gatekeeper I see: like the dust jacket of a brand-new book, the browns and oranges glowing in the summer sunshine. On sunny days in late July I have watched as the adults emerge en masse, dozens of them thronging the rhynes, before fluttering away to distant fields and gardens.

The gatekeeper's name refers to its habit of loitering alongside footpaths by the edges of fields, often close to stiles or gates. For the butterfly, this is the perfect place to live: with plenty of brambles, on whose small white and yellow flowers the adults feed; and patches of cock's-foot, fescues and other grasses, where they can lay their tiny, ivory-coloured eggs.

Like the meadow brown, the gatekeeper has two

prominent 'eyes' – one on each forewing – to confuse predators. On seeing the 'eye' a hungry bird may be fooled into pecking at the butterfly's wingtip rather than its body, which is why in late summer I often see both meadow browns and gatekeepers with part of their wingtips missing. Better to have a wonky flight-path than be dead, I suppose.

The third butterfly in the 'brown trio', the wall brown, was once a common sight on the Somerset Levels, but since the 1960s has more or less disappeared. As with so many other iconic grassland species, from the skylark to the cornflower, this is a result of half a century of so-called agricultural 'improvement'. The constant striving for higher yields, which can only be achieved by spraying the crops with a cocktail of pesticides, insecticides and herbicides, has turned much of lowland England into a sterile green desert.

Some creatures do still manage to hang on: on warm July days I have seen the marbled white butterfly, which, despite its name, is another member of the 'brown' family. Like its relatives, the marbled white is dependent on rough grassland, its striking piebald pattern easily picked out as it flits across the meadows in the midday sun. I have even seen marbled whites fluttering along nearby motorway verges, one of the few areas of grassland to escape the chemical onslaught.

❀

FOR THE LOCAL farmers, it has been a good year so far. In wet summers, the second crop of silage is sometimes not cut until the end of August; but this year the first crop was taken in early June, and now the grass is growing, albeit slowly, for the second crop. Perversely, after praying for – and getting – fine weather, my farming neighbours are now hoping it will rain.

Along the lanes, many of the verges have already been shorn of long grass, cow parsley and hogweed. Flocks of birds gather to feed on the spilt seeds: chaffinches and goldfinches, the odd reed bunting, and a pair of stock doves, all fly up as I walk past.

As a herd of cattle grazes slowly along the banks of the Perry Road rhyne, just two weeks after the summer solstice, I see the first sign of autumn. A small flock of birds passes overhead, heading directly south-east. Starlings: about forty of them, flying towards the RSPB reserve at Ham Wall. By late November, millions will descend on the reserve each evening, whirling through the darkening sky and delighting the watching crowds.

Although it is long before sunset, and swallows and swifts are still flying overhead, I still get the sense that the year has turned. The nights are gradually drawing in, and we are now nearer the end of the year than the beginning. The story of the parish and its wildlife, which until now has been one of anticipation, arrival and birth, has begun its gentle slide towards decline, departure and death.

Only then, in another turn of nature's wheel, will there be a rebirth.

❀

IN THE GARDEN, I see more signs of autumn. The first tiny, rock-hard apples are beginning to form: lime-green in colour, and still a long way from being eaten, cooked or turned into cider. Meanwhile, the hogweed is in rapid decline, its once creamy flower-heads now gone to seed. The meadow is awash with bindweed, its bell-shaped flowers forming a pleasing splash of white in the brownish-green landscape. Most gardeners despise this rampant flower, known as 'devil's guts' for its ability to propagate itself from the smallest fragment of root, but botanical writer Geoffrey Grigson took a more benevolent view:

> *Neither blasphemy, hoeing, nor selective weed-killers have yet destroyed it. One should speak kindly of its white and pink flowers, all the same.*

On sunny days the bindweed is visited by hordes of humming and buzzing insects. And another sound has been added to the summer soundtrack: the long, rough grass is filled with the calls of tiny field grasshoppers, which bounce all around me as I pass along the garden.

I've only just noticed that the brief season for

elderflowers is already over, the flower-heads rapidly darkening as they begin the process of turning into berries.
I remember my mother and I collecting the soft, creamy
blossoms, steeping them in boiling water, adding a pinch
or two of yeast and bottling the liquid in huge, gallon-sized
flagons. These would be left in the under-stairs cupboard
until autumn, when a cloudy yellow liquid the colour and
consistency of urine would be checked, filtered, tasted
and eventually pronounced to be an acceptable alternative to warm Liebfraumilch, the main drink of choice in
those days.

Later in the summer, towards the end of August, we
would collect the elderberries, too; heavy purple bunches,
crushed between our palms to release their deep magenta
juice. I was never tempted to eat them – they were said
to have a foul and bitter taste – but they did make a deep
red wine. Nowadays, even the cheapest supermarket
plonk would probably taste better, but it's a pity that our
modern drinking habits have lost the connection with the
land, and its bounty, that my mother's generation took for
granted.

Elder itself is a remarkable, if often overlooked, plant.
Neither bush nor tree, it has been described as 'the MDF
of the plant world', for its toughness, and 'nature's medicine chest', for its widespread uses in traditional medicine.
It has given rise to plenty of folklore, including the belief
that Christ's cross was made of elder wood. And back
in the seventeenth century, men driving cattle along the

droves to market are said to have cut themselves a stick of elder to ward away evil.

❁

AS THE HEAT intensifies through the long July days, it builds to a climax, before eventually releasing the tension with a summer thunderstorm. Signalling a change in the weather, swallows and house martins leave their nests and head skywards, gathering in large, twittering flocks. They fly just ahead of the rain clouds, where they pick off clusters of tiny insects to take back to their young. Sometimes they are joined by the more streamlined, scythe-like silhouettes of swifts, visitors from nearby towns and more distant cities. The swifts will soon disappear south, but the swallows and martins will linger here well into September, even perhaps October, before they and their offspring embark on their long and perilous journey to Africa.

Meanwhile, in our back garden, a permanent resident of the parish is busily feeding its hungry brood. A cider-apple tree is covered with white blossom, like icing on a wedding cake, hiding the trunk completely from view. But a chorus of cheeping sounds coming from this snow-white canopy demands a closer look. Halfway up the trunk I see a neat, oval-shaped hole; the worn, smooth, lighter patch of wood at its base showing that it is occupied by a brood of great spotted woodpeckers. Every couple of minutes I hear a loud and resonant 'chip', the signal that one of the parent birds is returning to the nest with food. Moments later it flies in, bouncing through the air on broad, rounded wings.

The male woodpecker usually lands a short distance above the nest hole, then manoeuvres himself into position before entering. A minute or so later he departs, having momentarily satisfied the hunger of his brood. He and his mate keep up their duties during every daylight hour for three frantic weeks, and even after the youngsters have left the nest, the parents will continue to feed them for another week or so.

The old name of this species was 'pied woodpecker', and its contrasting black-and-white plumage is certainly striking, as is the bright crimson patch on the back of the male's head. Great spotted woodpeckers have become much more common even in my lifetime, and now frequently visit garden bird-feeders, scaring off the smaller birds by their presence. They also raid nestboxes for baby blue tits, but despite this predatory behaviour the great spotted woodpecker has not yet joined the magpie on the blacklist of demonised garden birds.

In some ways it is surprising to find woodpeckers here at all in this flat, largely treeless landscape, where treecreepers are a rarity, and jays and nuthatches are absent. But there are enough clusters of oak and ash, especially around the houses and farms, to provide a refuge for them, along with the largest British member of its family, the green woodpecker.

About the size of a pigeon, the green woodpecker has yellow-and-green plumage, a scarlet crown, and large, staring eyes, making it impossible to mistake for any other bird. It is very partial to ants, and in summer can often be found feeding on the village lawns, pecking at the anthills in the longer grass to disturb their multitudinous occupants.

If my neighbours venture outdoors early in the morning, they may see this colourful bird heading off into the distance on clumsy, bouncing wings, and uttering the call that gave it its traditional country name, the 'yaffle'. My children, hearing this distant echoing sound, always refer to its maker as 'the woodpecker that laughs at us'.

❀

TWO OTHER KINDS of woodpecker used to live here in the parish, though sadly both are now long gone. The smallest European woodpecker, the lesser spotted, is virtually half the size of its great spotted relative; barely the length of a sparrow. True to its size, it behaves rather like a songbird, and in winter often joins flocks of tits as they travel around woods and hedgerows in search of food.

The lesser spotted woodpecker population boomed here in Somerset from the late eighteenth century onwards, after it was discovered that the process of cider-making caused drinkers to suffer from lead poisoning. Cider sales plummeted, but the orchards were left standing; with the trees' gradual decay providing the ideal breeding habitat for the lesser spotted woodpecker. In *Birds of Somersetshire*, published in 1869, Cecil Smith describes this species as being much more common than the great spotted, and as late as the 1920s, it was still considered to be the most numerous woodpecker in Somerset. Given its retiring habits, this means it must have been very common indeed.

By the end of the Second World War those ancient orchards had finally been grubbed up, and the lesser spotted woodpecker was beginning its rapid decline. My neighbour Mick remembers them nesting in the orchard alongside our home as recently as twenty years ago, but soon afterwards they had gone. The loss of elms, that classic tree of the English lowland landscape, was partly to blame; as was the close cutting of hedgerows, which the woodpeckers used as corridors to move around the neighbourhood.

Today, the lesser spotted woodpecker has disappeared not only from this parish, but from the whole of the Somerset Levels. This decline has been mirrored in the country as a whole, and there are now fewer than two thousand breeding pairs in Britain, mostly in our ancient woodlands. Even these are now under threat from a population explosion of the introduced muntjac deer, which browse the young saplings, destroying the breeding habitat for these, and many other, woodland birds.

A fourth species of woodpecker has disappeared not

only from this parish, and from the county of Somerset, but also from the whole of the British countryside. With a plumage like the bark of a tree, and the peculiar habit of twisting its neck and hissing at its enemies, the wryneck is a truly bizarre bird. It was once common enough to have acquired not only its vernacular name, but a wide range of folk names, including 'snake bird', 'twister' and 'emmet hunter', referring to its partiality for ants. But my favourite name for the wryneck is 'cuckoo's mate', so given because the wryneck used to arrive here in the middle of April, about the same time as the cuckoo.

The poet John Clare told the tale of a boy who disturbed a wryneck at its nest in a hollow tree; when the bird poked its head out of the hole and hissed, the boy assumed it was a snake, and fell to the ground in panic. Sadly such an experience is now denied the youngsters of this and every other English parish. A century ago the wryneck was common in orchards throughout southern England; but, like the lesser spotted woodpecker, it began to decline, this decline rapidly turning into freefall. The last pair bred in Somerset during the Second World War, and by the 1980s the wryneck had completely disappeared as a British breeding bird.

Another lost bird, the red-backed shrike, vanished at about the same time. Cecil Smith describes the shrike as common in Somerset, where it was known as the 'butcher bird', from its habit of impaling its prey – beetles, frogs and baby birds – on a thorn bush.

The reasons for the rapid and terminal decline of these two once widespread birds are still a mystery. It may have been the trend towards cooler, wetter summers; or perhaps the increased use of pesticides – we don't really know. I have seen the occasional wryneck and red-backed shrike along the east coast in autumn; migrants stopping off to rest and feed on their way from their Scandinavian breeding grounds to their African winter quarters. Red-backed shrikes have recently bred again in Britain, and may be on the verge of making a welcome comeback. But the wryneck appears to be lost to us for ever.

The story of the wryneck is not simply the tale of one vanishing species, but a parable about the devastating changes wrought on the British countryside in the past hundred years. For now that the orchard by my home – and every other orchard in England – no longer echoes with the wryneck's repetitive, high-pitched call, the whole landscape has not just been impoverished, but altered for ever. As with the cuckoo and the spotted flycatcher, this raises a pressing question: if those species our great-grandparents saw as part of their daily lives no longer survive here, does the place where we live merit the name countryside?

❀

BY JULY, THE waters of the parish – ditches, rhynes and cuts, carefully demarcated according to size – are thronged with life. Yet as I walk or cycle past, all I see is various shades of green: the dark, turbid carpet of blanket weed, ranging from near black to moss-green; and the paler, lime-green film of duckweed. Beneath this covering, below the water's surface, life is no doubt thriving.

Time for a spot of pond-dipping. As a child we did this all the time, though it wasn't such an organised activity as the term 'pond-dipping' suggests; we just went out with our nets and jam jars and fished for tiddlers. My own children are still at an age when they are both curious and enthusiastic in equal measure; the perfect time to investigate these hidden depths. And to help us do so, and identify what we find, we are accompanied by my naturalist friend Peter, whose knowledge of the inhabitants of our fresh waters is legion.

Most of the rhynes around here are steep-sided, the banks covered in brambles and nettles; good reasons to avoid them if we want to avoid pain, tears or soakings. But the concrete bridge over Mark Yeo, near the northern boundary of the parish, provides a firm platform, free from pricking or stinging plants. It also allows easy access for the nets: ours, a colourful selection bought for rock-pooling on beach holidays; Peter's the more professional version, a triangular muslin cone with a smooth, rosewood handle.

On this fine, sunny morning skylarks are singing, clumps of mayweed line the edges of the fields, and summer insects are already on the wing. A black-tailed skimmer dragonfly, his slender, powder-blue abdomen tipped with black, cruises low over the water; while matchstick-like azure damselflies flit from leaf to leaf. But the highlight is the presence of a most colourful and graceful insect: the banded demoiselle.

Banded demoiselles, which appear during warm, sunny days in June and July, are often mistaken for butter-flies or day-flying moths, and indeed another name for them is 'water-butterflies'. Today they live up to that description, fluttering delicately in little groups around the bankside vegetation, a foot or so above the surface of the water.

The dark bands across the transparent wings of the males flash constantly. They are presumably being used, like birdsong, to signal to rival males and potential mates. When the demoiselles land I am astonished by the colour of their abdomen, which varies according to the angle of the light: sometimes bottle-green, sometimes deep turquoise-blue. The female, though attractive in a quiet way, is easy to overlook as she perches on a reed stem. Her wings lack the male's dark band, and she is pea-green in colour, with a bright metallic sheen.

Beautiful as these insects are, we haven't come to look at wildlife above the surface, but below. The water itself is crystal clear, though the prevalence of blanket weed, jammed up against the dam of the concrete bridge, suggests that too much chemical fertiliser has been used on the adjacent fields. But the presence of pond snails on the weed's surface, each grazing its own little patch like slow-motion cattle out to grass, gives some cause for hope.

The surface of the water is alive with activity, another good sign. Mayflies are here, as are dozens of whirligig beetles, whizzing insanely around like dodgem cars, but never actually crashing into one another. Peter nets some, and we take a closer look: the black shell appearing almost silver, as if a small drop of mercury has been applied to its surface. The next pass of the net produces more treasures, which are swiftly transferred to a white metal dish, of the type we used to see in doctors' surgeries.

A leech swims around, alternately extending its front end and bunching up its rear, thus passing from a long, slender creature into a stout, round one, and back again, in a second or two. This effective means of locomotion continues when Peter picks it up, and we watch as it slides along his finger. The children are suitably entranced.

Water-boatmen are backstroke swimmers with three pairs of legs. They use the middle pair to propel them efficiently along (the rear legs are used as rudders, while the front pair grabs any passing morsels of food). We avoid picking them up, for they can give a nasty bite; as painful, Peter tells me, as a bee sting. We have also caught an awful lot of snails: the giant pond snail, whose elongated, spire-like shape neatly reflects the distant spire of the church at East Brent; and the smaller ramshorn snail, whose shell does indeed curl around itself like a sheep's horn. There is also a much smaller, reddish-black creature, which might pass for a tiny pebble: the cherrystone beetle, named for its obvious resemblance to the seeds of that summer fruit.

Meanwhile, Daisy and Charlie are catching fish by the netful: tiny silvery creatures rather like miniature white-bait. A closer look reveals three small spines – sticklebacks, of course. We explain the stickleback's extraordinary life-cycle to the children – how the males make a nest and look after the young – but they are more interested in catching even more fish. These include a few browner individuals without the spines: minnows.

George nets a great prize, a pale yellowish-brown crea-ture about the length of my thumb joint, with formidable-looking jaws. To me it looks like a dragonfly nymph, but Peter identifies it as the larva of the great diving beetle, which ranks with the largest British aquatic invertebrates. Deposited in the tray, it makes short work of grabbing and devouring a tiny stickleback.

A smaller rhyne, just across the road, is covered with lime-green: the run-of-the-mill common duckweed, and the larger giant duckweed, a deep auburn-red in colour. Duckweed's ability to completely cover the surface of the water, creating the illusion of solidity, has given rise to a chilling folk tale: the story of Jenny Greenteeth. Jenny is supposed to lure little children into her watery lair by tempting them to walk on the solid-looking duckweed, causing them to fall through and drown. My own children watch agog as I relate this story, presumably designed to warn earlier generations of the perils of venturing too near the water.

After a pint and a ploughman's at the White Horse Inn, we head across to Tealham Moor, where a herd of curious cattle wanders over to watch our equally curious antics. Here we find no fewer than four out of five species of native duckweed: the pale green ivy-leaved, and the bladder-like gibbous, making up the quartet. It is the fifth, more elusive duckweed species we are really searching for: the tiny *Wolffia arrhiza*, the smallest flowering plant in Britain, and one of the smallest in the world. As its scientific name suggests, this plant has no roots, and being so tiny, is not an easy plant to find. But Peter has a cunning plan. Turning his net around, he dips the rosewood handle into the water and sweeps it from side to side. Duckweed sticks to wood, so hopefully his trawl will include our tiny target.

Unfortunately, despite persistent sweeping, it does not. As we walk back along the banks of the rhyne we do come across the open shell of a huge duck mussel; at almost 5 inches across, a giant compared with most British invertebrates. The outside of the shell is greenish-yellow, marked with narrow black lines, while the inside has the smooth, polished appearance of mother-of-pearl. Our fascination with the mussel shell means we fail to notice the cattle approaching; and a brief moment of panic ensues as the children look up to see a wall of black and white towering over them. A swift clamber over the farm gate, and our outing reaches a satisfactory conclusion.

Very satisfactory, indeed. The children's verdict – 'the best day ever!' – suggests that the rival attractions of TV and computer games may not be quite as compelling as we sometimes suppose. Given the simple pleasures of a fishing net, clear water and some of the most fascinating creatures on the planet, children actually find nature quite interesting, after all.

※

RIVALLING THE FOX as the least popular animal around these parts is the badger. This is not the place to go into the debate about badgers and bovine TB, but of one thing there can be no doubt: the badger is never going to come top of the animal hit parade, at least among the local farming community here in Somerset. But among many other people, in the country and the city, badgers are very popular indeed. Thanks to television programmes such as *Springwatch*, and the genial old character in *The Wind in the Willows*, badgers are often regarded as rather amiable creatures, to be encouraged rather than condemned or culled.

So which of these two images – the 'good badger' and the 'bad badger' – is the right one? Of course the truth lies somewhere in between: the badger is simply a wild animal getting on with its life as best it can, given that human beings have invaded its world. For badgers are, above all, creatures of habit. They live in the same setts as their ancestors, follow the same nocturnal trails in search of food, and remain faithful to the same place, even if people have changed it beyond recognition; for example, by building a housing estate over it.

My in-laws, living in a bungalow on the outskirts of Wedmore, are currently fighting a running battle to stop the badgers digging up their small, neat lawn. It's a battle that, despite yards of chicken wire being mobilised as a defence, they may well lose: it takes a lot to stop a determined badger. But others welcome the presence of badgers in their back garden, and even seek to attract them there.

Susie and Kev live just outside the village of East Brent, a quarter-hour's walk to the north-west of the parish, and at the foot of our well-known local landmark, Brent Knoll. This volcano-shaped hill rises almost 500 feet above the surrounding landscape, and over the centuries has played host to an Iron Age hill fort, a Roman camp, and a pitched battle between the men of Somerset and the invading Danes, a battle the local army won. It is also home to an extensive clan of badgers, which have become regular visitors to Susie and Kev's back garden.

Until I moved down to Somerset, I had only ever seen two badgers in my whole life: both at night, both while I was driving, and both very brief views, as they scuttled across the road in front of me, a frustrating flash of black, white and grey. For despite their size – about the same as a fox terrier – badgers are just as elusive as any other wild mammal. Since living here I have enjoyed a few more encounters with them, such as one lumbering across a frosty field early one winter's morning, or a rear end disappearing down the lane as we returned home from a late night out. But these have always been rather brief and unsatisfactory, so I am looking forward to a more rewarding experience tonight.

And a more rewarding experience, with badgers at least, would be hard to find. As I approach the front door it opens, and Susie quickly beckons me in. It's not yet ten o'clock, and still fairly light, but the animals are, apparently, already here. She ushers me into the sitting room, and through the French windows I can see a bulky male badger shambling across the lawn, vacuuming up peanuts at an impressive rate.

Within a few minutes, as it gets dark, he is joined by the whole clan: four cubs and three females, eight badgers in all. Susie tells me they first arrived during the winter snows, taking advantage of the food she was putting out for the birds. Since then they've become regular visitors, and now that the summer drought has turned the ground rock-hard, and worms and slugs are hard to find, they appear grateful for her ready supply of nuts and jam-and-peanut-butter sandwiches. As I watch, they move steadily across the lawn, grazing intently like a herd of cattle.

The more I look at badgers, the more they strike me as odd. They are mustelids – the same family as otters, weasels and stoats – but all these animals have a recognisable kinship with one another, reflected in their long, slender shape and sleek appearance. In contrast, badgers are stout, short-tailed, with that huge head and unmistakable black-and-white pattern. Looked at more closely, they strike me as having more in common with anteaters or armadillos than any native British mammal.

They range slowly and deliberately back and forth across the clover-covered lawn; one, bolder animal venturing onto the patio, so close I can no longer focus my binoculars. The cubs are almost the size of their parents now, but still retain their playful manner.

An hour or so after they first appeared, the badgers trail off, one by one, into the nearby woods. For the rest of the night they will forage for whatever they can find. But whatever they discover, it is unlikely to be as convenient as what's on offer on Susie and Kev's back lawn.

❁

BY THE MIDDLE of July, the world is rapidly turning purple. Along the parish verges, the yellows, creams and whites of spring have given way to the mauves, lilacs and violets of summer. These richer, fuller, deeper shades suit this time of plenty, at the very moment in the calendar when every plant and animal is busy fulfilling its biological destiny.

They look pretty too, these varied visions of floral excess. Purple loosestrife, the undisputed queen of that shade, is in full bloom along the edges of the rhynes and ditches, heavy with colour. It is known locally as 'water vinny'; another folk name is 'long purples', which could hardly be bettered for this statuesque wild flower, standing tall and proud in the damper areas of the parish throughout July.

On the drier ground between, there are tight clumps of creeping thistle: tall, slender, with a tuft of white hairs perched on top of the dull purple head; and a larger but equally spiky plant, the teasel. Unlike the familiar deep brown objects my grandmother kept in her favourite vase, these are in flower, not seed; and pale green, with a light dusting of purple across their spines. Teasels were once grown commercially, being used to clean and comb cloth, as their fine, sharp spines were far more effective than anything we could artificially manufacture.

But the most common floral purple, found along almost every lane and drove, is the great willowherb. Its delicate pinkish-purple flowers, clustered atop tall, green, hairy stalks, provide a new layer of colour between road and hedgerow. Like so many familiar summer flowers, it has many country names, in this case sharing a theme. 'Apple-pie', 'coddled apples', 'custard-cups', 'currant-dumpling' and 'codlins-and-cream', all refer to a link with fruit-based puddings – 'codlins' being sour apples that were boiled in milk.

For more than three hundred years, since the seventeenth-century botanist John Ray claimed to have crushed the leaves and smelt apples, books repeated this anecdote as an explanation of these fruity folk names. But Geoffrey Grigson pointed out that the leaves and flowers of the great willow-herb 'have no characteristic smell'. I rub them between my fingers, and discover that he is quite correct; they are virtually scentless. Still, it is a pretty flower, adding a welcome splash of colour to the increasingly brown-and-yellow scene.

What is missing is the great willowherb's cousin, rosebay willowherb. The Americans call this familiar plant fireweed, for its ability to colonise newly burned or cleared ground. Known for its sudden appearance on bomb sites during the Second World War, it has now spread throughout Britain along roadside verges and railway embankments, using the slipstream of passing traffic to spread its seeds. Rosebay willowherb is a common sight along the nearby M5 and A38, but is not found along the more lushly vegetated roadsides of this parish.

There is some dispute about whether or not rosebay willowherb is an alien plant, but my final vision of purple certainly is. At this time of year almost every garden in the village boasts its very own buddleia bush, whose purple pyramids are bursting out of its dense green foliage. Originally from the Himalayan foothills, buddleia was brought to Britain in the late-Victorian era, and soon spread via gardens and waste ground. With buddleia, of course, come butterflies: and, as befits its brash, exotic nature, brash, exotic ones. Today a peacock butterfly perches on one of the flower-heads, greedily sucking up the juicy nectar with his delicate proboscis.

I am momentarily transfixed by his beauty: the rich orange upperwings, with their startling 'eyes', contrasting with the sooty black underwings, the perfect camouflage should it need to hide. As I watch, a movement at the corner of my eye draws my attention. Another insect is moving rapidly across my line of vision; and finally, the realisation of what I am looking at begins to dawn. The synapses click into place, and I feel my face crack into a smile. For this vision of beauty whizzing back and forth before my eyes is none other than a hummingbird hawkmoth.

Of all the wild creatures I had hoped to see within the borders of the parish, the hummingbird hawkmoth is at the top of the list. Just consider its life story. Sometime earlier this spring, this little insect set off from its birthplace, somewhere in North Africa or southern Spain. It flew north, a distance of some 1,500 miles, before finally making landfall here in Britain. Now, on this fine, sunny day in the middle of July, it has chosen to feed on the buddleia bush in my very own garden.

I watch as it zooms to and fro, hovering momentarily by each flower-head, extending its proboscis to feed, then moving a few inches up, down, left or right. I have watched hummingbirds many times in the Americas, and the hummingbird hawkmoth really does rival them in the flying department. Convergent evolution truly is a remarkable thing.

I look even closer, and study its subtle shades and features. The 'tail' (the rear of the abdomen) is dark brown above with white sides, while the body is a paler greyish-brown colour, with a soft, furry texture. Large, staring eyes give the creature the appearance of a small mammal, rather than an insect. Its wings, held at an angle above its body, whirr back and forth so fast I can only just see the pale orange patch on their rear edge. And that long, black proboscis is constantly searching for nectar, to provide the energy it needs to keep up this astonishing performance.

I wonder why the hawkmoth doesn't just follow the example of the peacock butterfly, and stay put for a while. But its strategy is one of perpetual motion rather than rest, and it works very well. The hummingbird hawkmoth is a highly successful and widespread species, found from Portugal in the west to Japan in the east, and in a good summer as far north as Scandinavia.

It is also seen increasingly often here in Britain, with surprised householders often convinced that they have seen a real hummingbird feeding on their garden flowers. But while I am delighted to see this exquisite creature, especially in my own little patch of airspace, I am concerned about the reason why it is here. There can be little doubt that the hawkmoth's recent northward spread is due to the effects of global climate change. It may well benefit from this; other, equally special creatures, may not.

As the hummingbird hawkmoth flicks his wings a little

harder than before, and disappears over the elder hedge and away, I suppress these gloomy thoughts, and simply celebrate the few glorious moments we have shared.

❀

ANOTHER MIGRANT INSECT is famed for its occasional mass invasions; and in the summer of 2009, we experienced the greatest of these for many years. The delightfully named painted lady butterfly is a softer-coloured, more orange version of the familiar red admiral. And just like the red admiral it is a migrant, travelling all the way to our shores from Spain and North Africa.

But unlike the red admiral, it is far from a regular visitor. Some years we see only a few; in others, they arrive in their thousands. Or, as in 2009, in their tens of millions. That year I noticed my first painted lady at the very end of May, when I came across one feeding in my garden. Over the next couple of months, I saw thousands of them, usually whizzing across at eye level, here one moment, gone the next, as they headed on north.

On the very same day that I saw my first painted lady, the newspapers ran the story that Britain was experiencing the biggest mass migration of this enigmatic butterfly since the 1960s, and possibly since records began. They had been spotted coming in off the sea at Portland Bill in Dorset a week earlier; and within a few days had arrived in force. Later in the summer, reports suggested that with each butterfly laying 300 eggs, by early August there could be more than a billion painted ladies in the country.

This may have been an exaggeration, yet there is no doubt that during that memorable summer the painted lady was by far the most abundant butterfly in Britain. By September, numbers were falling rapidly, and by October they had all but disappeared, though sightings of them heading south, out to sea across the English Channel, proved that some, at least, were attempting to return whence they had come.

The painted lady year aside, for a few weeks each late June and early July we are in what a naturalist friend of mine calls 'the butterfly gap'. This is the period between spring butterflies such as the orange-tip, that reach peak numbers in April and May, and those that don't emerge until July, such as the gatekeeper. But now, from the middle of July onwards, they are back with a vengeance: as well as meadow browns and gatekeepers, there are fresh broods of commas and peacocks, so that on a sunny day there may be ten different species on the wing in my garden alone.

One of these looks, at first sight, like a darker version of the male meadow brown. It is, in fact, a ringlet: an un-assuming denizen of the woodland edge, with dark, velvety smooth upperwings and brown underwings, each dotted with a series of what my son George calls 'hula hoops': the tiny cream rings that give this butterfly its name.

❀

EACH SUMMER THE village is invaded; not, this time, by migrating birds or butterflies, but by a group of noisy, exuberant, but good-natured children. They have come from a deprived part of south Bristol, which even though it is less than thirty miles away, might as well be on another planet. These seven- to eleven-year-olds are here for a week, thanks to the Avalon Camps scheme, which gives them the chance of a holiday in the country.

My neighbour Jon and his team of eager volunteers run the camp with just the right balance of discipline and friendly encouragement. The children enjoy sports and games, drawing and model-making, quizzes, barbecues, songs and stories, and a final-night concert. And, thanks to an uncharacteristic willingness to volunteer on my part, nature study.

Soon after daybreak on a late-July morning, I am on the edge of a field behind the church hall, opening a moth trap. The selection is not quite as impressive as earlier in the season, as the hawkmoths have now disappeared, but it is still colourful and varied enough to interest the children. Among our haul is a single female ghost swift, with a more orangey-yellow hue than the male I saw back in June. The children look suitably impressed.

After breakfast we head out into the wilds of Shapwick Heath, where the children can really let off steam. Given a selection of nets and plastic containers, and the freedom to run around catching any insect they can find, they reveal their true nature. They are no longer 'deprived kids', or whatever label has been given them in the past, but just kids, showing the enthusiasm for the natural world that all children possess, but rarely get the chance to indulge. They have lightning-quick instincts, and catch a far bigger selection of creatures than I could manage. I do have to discourage them from collecting too many white-lipped snails, which being abundant, varied and easy to get, fill up the boxes pretty quickly.

Two hours later, they pile back onto their coach, having rather reluctantly released their quarry back into the wild. I go home and lie down, drained by their sheer energy, but also deeply fulfilled. The whole experience confirms my belief that if we could only get our nation's children out and about, encountering nature on their own terms, we would solve many of the problems currently besetting today's youngsters; and perhaps create a whole new generation of naturalists.

❀

AN HOUR BEFORE dusk on a warm, muggy evening at the end of the month, a cold front approaches from the northwest, bringing a rapidly freshening breeze. The swallows are on the wing, hawking for insects among the newly sheared sheep. Their short tails and erratic, jerky movements show these are recently fledged youngsters, just out of their nests in the nearby barns. They need to test those wings, for in not much more than two months' time they will be using them for a very long journey indeed.

Further along the road, a busy farmyard is home to more swallows, along with a species of bird that has lived alongside human beings for even longer: the house sparrow. A male sits on the telegraph wire, tail cocked, while a few yards away, on the farm gate, a female trembles her wings. She looks like a young bird, begging for food; but in this case her begging has a more basic purpose, to entice the male to fly down to mate with her.

There are good numbers of sparrows here, certainly compared to many other parts of Britain. But when I quiz Rick he tells me that, back in the 1960s and 70s, he used to see sparrows here in huge flocks, with well over a thousand birds in each. I recall that when I was growing up on the outskirts of London, at about the same time, vast flocks of sparrows were a common sight.

Seeing the sparrows and swallows together reminds me of the day, a few years ago, when we first arrived at our new home. It was, I recall, the hottest day of the hottest month ever recorded in Britain. As I emerged from the packed car after a long and tiring journey, the very first sound I heard was the familiar chirping of a house sparrow. And the first bird I saw, shooting overhead in the clear blue sky a moment later, was a swallow. For me, these two species symbolise the polar opposites of life here in the parish: one an unpretentious bird that stays put, the other a showy acrobat that travels the globe, racking up thousands of miles in its short but eventful lifetime.

AUGUST

Augustus marks the height of summer: long, hot, sunny days, the hum of bumblebees, and the daily traffic jam along the motorway, as holidaymakers head south-west on their annual migration to the beaches of Devon and Cornwall. During the evenings and weekends, the sportier villagers gather to bat and bowl at the cricket club to the rear of the White Horse Inn. Preparations are also well under way for the main event in the village calendar: Harvest Home.

But although we still have a month or more of fine weather to look forward to, one of our star summer visitors has already headed away from the parish airspace, to new oceans of blue. The swifts, which cut through the summer air like test pilots, have gone; leaving only an echo of their banshee screams, the memory fading with every passing day.

Almost all of Britain's 80,000 pairs of swifts are now well on their way south, crossing the Mediterranean Sea and the Sahara Desert before spending the winter in Central Africa. For a bird that habitually flies 500 miles or more a day when here in Britain, this journey presents few problems. Feeding on tiny flying insects as they go, they spend more than half the year under African skies, before returning at the end of April or in the first few days of May.

Given that swifts are with us for just three months, it is extraordinary what a hold they have on our consciousness.

This is a bird of superlatives: a bird that can catch 100,000 insects in a single day, stay airborne for as long as four years, and travel more than a million miles during its lifetime. We think about swifts even during their long absence, so that on a warm, sunny day in late April I find myself gazing at the skies, willing them to return.

Now that the swifts have departed, the end of the summer is in sight. The days are getting imperceptibly shorter, birdsong is beginning to fade, and intimations of mortality are all around us.

Not that our other iconic summer visitor would endorse this view. Over to the west of the parish, in a cluster of industrial units, half a dozen pairs of swallows are busily collecting food for their second broods. Every minute or two, they bring little balls of tiny flying insects back to the nest. I duck as the birds swoop low past my head, even though I know their piloting skills mean there is no danger of a collision. From inside I can hear the soft twittering of the youngsters, whose volume rises each day, as they begin to outgrow their flimsy nest of mud, straw, grass and feathers. It won't be long before this brood leave the nest and join their well-grown siblings on the telegraph wires outside. And in less than two months they will flick their wings, drop off the wires and float away, south, to join the swifts in Africa.

❀

OF ALL BRITAIN'S butterflies, my favourites are the blues. They are a dazzling array of beauty in miniature – even the large blue is small by butterfly standards. Many of our blue butterflies can only be found on what is confusingly called 'unimproved' grassland – habitats that have never been ploughed, sprayed, or planted with crops. Such places – mainly on chalk and limestone soils – are as rare as hen's teeth in the modern British countryside, so the ranges of most of these butterflies are fairly limited.

But on warm, sunny days in August, two species of blue butterfly do visit my garden, sometimes in good numbers. The common blue and the brown argus are never very obvious, being so much smaller and less showy than the peacocks, red admirals and commas that dominate this late-summer season. They are also less active, perching to feed on a thistle-head or clump of meadowsweet, rather than flitting about like their more exhibitionist cousins.

Take a closer look, though, and their appeal becomes clear. The larger of the two, the common blue, has a slightly looser, floppier flight than its relative. When it lands, it may momentarily open its wings to reveal a fine, pale blue shade, as if someone has sprinkled a thin layer of microscopic particles over their surface. The female is less striking than the male, and browner in hue, though a bluish tinge can usually be seen as she turns towards the sun.

But my favourite of these summer butterflies is the brown argus, named after the giant with a hundred eyes in Greek mythology. Small and neat, measuring barely an inch from one wingtip to the other, the rich, chocolate-brown of its wings is set off by a series of tiny, jagged orange arrow-heads along their sides, and the snow-white border beyond. When it closes its wings, as it usually does when feeding, it reveals a series of egg-shaped blobs, the tiny 'eyes' to which its name refers.

When I first saw a brown argus in my garden, one warm August evening a few years ago, I was surprised. This is a chalkland specialist, laying its eggs on the common rock-rose, and I never imagined it could fly the few miles from the slopes of the Mendips to reach these low-lying lands on the levels. But males, in particular, have a reputation for 'going flyabout' on warm summer days; a strategy which has enabled it to colonise new areas of downland and grassland, and to extend its range north and west. Unlike some more sedentary species of butterfly, the brown argus looks set to take advantage of global warming during the coming decades.

❀

ON A FINE, sunny day in early August, the breeze blows the thistledown up into the air, the croak of the raven and the mew of the buzzard echo in the distance, and on the lawn, a green woodpecker searches for newly emerged colonies of flying ants, picking up dozens at a time with its long, sticky tongue.

Small copper butterflies join the blues and browns, seeking out nectar on a clump of meadowsweet. Migrant hawker, emperor and common darter dragonflies patrol along the path through the meadow as efficiently as border guards, hunting down flying insects as they go. Grasshoppers and crickets forage for food in the long grass below, quietly humming to each other. And a single red-tailed bumblebee, whose furry black body looks like a guardsman's black busby with an orange-red trim, floats from flower to flower.

The red-tailed is eye-catching among the several different kinds of bumblebee that ply their quiet trade in the hedgerows, gardens and roadsides of the parish, from early spring until late autumn. Other common varieties include the buff-tailed, usually the first to emerge on fine warm days in February or March, and the white-tailed. We are also home to several species of 'cuckoo-bee', which, like their avian namesake, lay their eggs in other bees' nests. They can be told apart from their hosts by the lack of pollen sacs on their hind legs; they have no need of these, as they get the other bees to do the hard work of raising their young for them.

The name bumblebee is often assumed to derive from these bulky insects' rather uncertain, bumbling flight-paths; but it actually comes from the sound they make. Indeed their original name, and the standard usage until at least the 1920s, was 'humblebees'. 'Humble' has nothing to do with humility, but again refers to their low, humming sound. Like their domesticated cousin the honeybee, bumblebees have had a rough time lately. A combination of chemical farming, habitat loss, wet summers and climate change all threaten the survival of these vivid insects. But for the moment at least, on a warm August day, the gardens of the parish are alive with them.

❀

THE FRUIT TREES and bushes around the edge of our garden are beginning to show the results of the summer's fine weather. Plums and apples – for eating, cooking and making cider – ripen and swell on the trees, while the elder and blackthorn bushes are covered with inky-black berries and sloes.

But above all, it's baby-bird time. I say baby, although the vast majority have long since left the safety and comfort of their nest, and begun to make their way in the world. At the far end of our garden, the dense foliage of the hawthorns and blackthorns, and the tall ash trees, provide excellent cover for these vulnerable youngsters. Fledgling great tits, their yellow cheeks giving away their youth, potter about the foliage, as do juvenile chiffchaffs, their neat, fresh plumage a sharp contrast to that tatty appearance of their exhausted parents.

A robin hops out and cocks his head, staring at me with one beady eye. His orange breast would mark him out as an adult, were it not for the state of his headdress;

from the neck upwards he still retains the speckled brown of his juvenile plumage. A young blackbird also sports a cinnamon-coloured head above his black body, as he pecks away furtively at the ripening purple sloes.

Bramble, elder, hawthorn and blackthorn are all readily giving up their fruit as a crafty sacrifice to the birds. The fleshy fruit may be digested, but the hard seed remains intact, until the usual processes of nature see it coming out at the other end from where it went in. This increases the plants' chances of spreading, as birds fly off to new places beyond their reach.

At this time of year, the berries attract not just thrushes and blackbirds, but a whole suite of species whose usual diet is insects. Migrants such as the whitethroat, willow warbler, chiffchaff and blackcap will soon be heading south for the winter, and now need fuel for their travels. So when the berries reach their peak, they supplement their diet with these fleshy, energy-rich fruits, enabling them to build up deposits of fat vital for the long journey ahead.

One small clump of elder and hawthorn bushes to the back of our house has, since we first arrived here, attracted more than twenty different species of bird. These range from wood pigeons, collared doves and great spotted woodpeckers, through thrushes, blackbirds, finches and sparrows, to no fewer than six species of warbler. We once even saw an escaped blue-crowned parakeet – originally from South America – until constant mobbing by the local jackdaws forced him to fly away.

Later in the month, my favourite berry-eating bird usually turns up: the lesser whitethroat. Having skulked away in the parish hedgerows all summer, the only evidence of its presence being that soft, almost inaudible song, this neat little warbler finally emerges in late August and early September. Two or three lesser whitethroats appear on the elder each year, sporting their neat, new shades of grey and white, and picking off the deep, blackish-purple berries one at a time. If I approach them carefully they may allow me momentarily into their lives. But they don't stay long: within a few days they head off eastwards on that epic journey via northern Italy, the Balkans and the Middle East, to their wintering grounds in West Africa.

❀

ANOTHER BIRD SMALL enough to overlook has also turned up in my garden. Slender and buffish-brown, with a distinctively upright posture and delicate streaks on his upper breast, it perches at the top of a cider-apple tree, occasionally flitting out on long, slender wings, in a tentative exploratory flight. It is a young spotted flycatcher, the first I have ever seen in the garden or, come to that, in the parish.

Arriving in mid-May, and departing in August or September, the spotted flycatcher is here for barely three months; its stay coinciding with the warmest, sunniest period of the year. Flycatchers were once the quintessential birds of the English rural summer, coming to breed in walled gardens and churchyards throughout the countryside. Here, amid flower borders and croquet lawns, they would build their nests, deep in the foliage of climbing plants or tucked into crevices in brickwork.

But since my childhood, spotted flycatcher numbers have dropped by well over three-quarters, so a bird that was once a common and familiar summer visitor has now become a very infrequent sight indeed. As with the cuckoo and the turtle dove, problems on its West African wintering grounds are the main reason for this precipitous decline, although a run of wet summers at home has not helped.

So will this turn out to be a valedictory sighting – my last in the parish, as well as my first? Will the spotted flycatcher follow the wryneck and the red-backed shrike into terminal decline, followed by extinction as a British breeding bird? And in a few decades' time, will the fact that it was once a common sight in country villages every-where seem bizarre? Or, perhaps, this unpretentious bird will win an eleventh-hour reprieve, and continue to delight us with its presence – its time here spanning, and in some ways symbolising, the brief English summer.

❀

THE MIDDLE OF August also sees that vital event in the parish year, Harvest Home. Based on the traditional harvest suppers that have taken place since the land was first used to grow crops and raise livestock, the event we attend today is a late-Victorian invention, but more than a century of tradition has been enough to cement its place in village life.

The first signs of Harvest Home appear, like foxgloves, in the middle of July: home-made wooden placards giving the date (the second Saturday in August), the venue (Rick's field, next door to my home) and, most importantly, the name of the tribute band scheduled to appear at this year's concert. With a week or so to go before the big day, marquees are erected, food and drink prepared, and the schedule finalised. On the day itself, a combination of military precision, hard work and years of experience means things always run smoothly, no matter what.

Following a church service of thanksgiving, more than three hundred people from the village and beyond sit down to a simple but satisfying lunch, followed by a series of speeches, some commendably brief, others not. The afternoon is given over to the village children, who enjoy games, tea and mountains of buns; as well as the rival attractions of a small funfair. The next morning, hangovers not withstanding, clearing and dismantling begins; and by the following Monday you would hardly know the event had taken place at all.

The continued popularity of Harvest Home reflects the importance of farming to the parish. In 1791, John Collinson wrote:

*The lands are rich, and in general valuable, and
there are many small dairy and grazing farms.*

Five years later, the agricultural historian John Billingsley
waxed even more lyrical about the fertility of this part of
the country:

> *The plains are remarkable for their luxuriant
> herbiage, which furnishes not only a sufficiency for its
> own consumption, but also a considerable surplus
> for other markets: London, Bristol, Salisbury, and
> other parts of the kingdom, are annually supplied
> with fat oxen, sheep and hogs, together with cyder,
> cheese, butter, and many other articles, in great
> abundance.*

Today, although there are more than thirty farms marked
on the most recent Ordnance Survey map of the parish,
only about half are still working. Back in 1851, though,
the census listed more than seventy farms in the parish,
most of them less than fifty acres in area. These were, as
you might expect from this lush, wet area, mainly dairy
farms producing milk, butter and cheese; although sheep,
pigs and poultry were also kept in good numbers. These
animals – and the meat they produced – were fuelled
by the main crop of the parish: hay. Even in the 1950s
haymaking was still a common sight, and one villager
recalls that any ricks left untouched the following spring

would be colonised by nesting birds. Today, it's almost all silage.

The other major crop was, of course, apples; still used to make Somerset's traditional drink, cider. Cider-making dates back at least to the thirteenth century (and probably far longer). The boom time for planting orchards was the second half of the seventeenth century and the early years of the eighteenth. In those days, cider was mainly for drinking at home rather than for commercial sale, using long-forgotten varieties of apple with wonderfully evocative names: Royal Wilding, Flood-Hatch, Woodcock, Red-Hedge Pip, Old Jerfey and Redstreak. Odd clumps of cider-apple trees still grow in gardens all over the parish, including my own. Their fruit is pale, bitter and, unfortunately, completely inedible.

❀

A LIGHT SUMMER shower passes overhead, briefly heightening my forgotten sense of smell, as the dust on the lane is battered by raindrops and bursts into the air. It's a hard scent to describe – with a warm, toasty quality, yet also a harsh, metallic top note that betrays its tarmac origins. The shower is not enough to stop the butterflies: speckled woods, large whites and common blues still bounce from flower to flower, only occasionally knocked off course by a particularly heavy drop of rain. The swallows and house martins also continue to fly, skirting around the edge of the shower as it passes across the parish.

Since my last visit in the early spring, the churchyard has burst into leaf, the trees providing ideal hiding places for many young birds, newly fledged from the various nesting places around the church. A quartet of pied wagtails flit across the smooth grass around the grave-stones, stopping from time to time to pick off tiny morsels of insect food with their slender bills. One balances precariously on the crenellated rooftop of the old village school, still coming to terms with its new-found ability to use its tail as a rudder.

The calls of coal tits, goldcrests and chiffchaffs pipe unseen from the evergreen foliage of the yews, but there is no sign of the spotted flycatchers that bred here back in June. All has changed: most of these birds weren't even alive at the start of this year. Yet one permanent feature, almost as old as the church itself, remains: the lichens. Grey, green and mustard-yellow encrustations throng every stone surface in sight, living at a different timescale to the frantic lifespan of the birds, and indeed at a different timescale to our own, comparatively brief, lives.

'The Dead in Christ shall rise first', proclaims one Victorian gravestone. Perhaps so; but if and when they do, the lichens will certainly be around to witness the miracle.

❀

Colour and sound have been seeping out of the countryside; so slowly and gradually I barely noticed until now. Along the narrow border between lane and ditch, where reed warblers sang until a few weeks ago, the colour has all but gone. The yellows and whites of April and May, and the pinks and purples of June and July, have mostly turned to browns, buffs and greens, as the plants of the parish set seed in readiness for the coming autumn. Only the odd clump of purple loosestrife provides a respite from this semi-monochrome vision, and even this majestic flower is gradually losing its shade as the flowers turn to seeds, from the bottom to the top of each long, floral finger.

If I am looking for colour, I must either search more carefully, or learn to appreciate more subtle shades: the deep magenta-brown of the drooping reed-heads, the pale grey-green of the underside of willow leaves as they turn in the wind, and the small splashes of red, and occasionally purple, on the low bramble bushes, the first ripe blackberries of the year. Aurally, our world is diminished, too. The spring soundtrack of birdsong and buzzing insects has given way to the persistent whistle of a south-westerly breeze. The occasional call of a chiffchaff, and the chacking of distant jackdaws, are the only natural sounds I hear.

The field alongside Mark Yeo, which only a month or so ago was filled with the tinkling calls of linnets and goldfinches as they stripped the seeds from the sorrel and meadow barley, has been cut, and is now being grazed by a herd of black-and-tan-coloured cattle. The water itself is surprisingly clear, apart from the usual carpet of blanket weed jammed up against the bridge by the prevailing winds. The pale green surface is broken only by the occasional discarded plastic fertiliser bag.

I search in vain for two elusive creatures of the parish waterways: the kingfisher and the water vole. Kingfishers I do occasionally see, usually in the winter months, when their need to feed during the short daylight hours makes them more active and conspicuous. Water voles remain a closed book to me; I know they are here, but have yet to see them. The sign that marks the beginning of Vole Road, which I pass frequently on my travels, mocks me for my efforts.

Today the only sign of life is a party of low-flying swallows, skirting an inch or so above the surface to grab unseen flying insects, before changing course at the very last moment with a whip of their long, blue wings, to avoid crashing into a low bridge. Then a strident, scolding sound from the vegetation at the edge of the rhyne is followed by the hasty appearance of a moorhen, jerking indignantly as it walks away across the surface of the duckweed, its long green toes just managing to bear its weight on this porridge-like surface.

The moorhen may be taken for granted but it is one of Britain's most attractive waterbirds. It doesn't have the grandeur of a swan, fly spectacularly like wild geese, or stage the breathtaking courtship display of the great crested grebe, but it is nevertheless a beauty. This is a particularly fine specimen: its bright red beak tipped with custard-yellow, and a snowy white flash beneath its tail, easily visible as it walks away from me. The bird's body, although it appears black or dark brown at a distance, is a subtle mixture of deep blue, chestnut, purple and chocolate-brown, set off with a raggedy cream stripe along its flanks. A poet friend of mine called it the 'single drop of blood in the darkest night bird', which sums it up rather well.

One of two common British representatives of the rail family – the other being the equally ignored coot – the moorhen has adapted extraordinarily well to its chosen habitat of tiny patches of water. Ponds, puddles and, in this parish, rhynes are the moorhen's favoured habitat; one it rarely has to share with any other bird. It is also a very sedentary bird: at the height of the hard winter, the furthest our local moorhens managed to move was to the top of the bank of the rhyne, a distance of a few feet. Perhaps it is this parochialism – the way the moorhen is faithful to these modest village watercourses rather than distant rivers and lakes – which so endears it to us.

Baby moorhens are even more appealing: little black balls of fluff with a hint of the adult's red and yellow around their head and bill, and hilariously out-of-proportion feet. As they fledge, they turn into one of the gawkiest juvenile birds of all – a classic example of a cute baby turning into an awkward teenager – before finally attaining the subtle allure of the adult.

The name moorhen is, when you think about it, rather puzzling. It is actually a corruption of 'mere-hen': bird of the meres, or shallow lakes. It has occurred to me that the name for this part of the world, the Somerset Moors and Levels, may also have derived from this same root: 'meres and levels' certainly makes more sense in this flat, wet landscape. Local names for the moorhen include 'water hen', while a Somerset name no longer in use, 'skitty hen', refers to the bird's habit of dashing off across surface vegetation when disturbed, as I have just witnessed.

Further along Vole Road there is a much smaller baby moorhen, just a few days old and now faced with a race to grow before the autumn frosts make food more difficult to find, reducing its chances of survival. A kestrel flies low overhead, causing the chick and its parent to panic. Imagine what it must be like to live in this steep-sided rhyne, the only view a grassy bank on either side, and the sky above; a sky which can bring danger, even death, at a moment's notice. No wonder the mother moorhen looks so nervous.

❀

A WEEK OF rain towards the end of the month has produced a small, muddy puddle in the corner of the field behind our home. Despite the competing attractions of rhynes, ditches and, not so far away, lakes, the five cygnets that hatched out here at the end of June have chosen this as their playground. Under the ever-watchful eyes of their parents, they wallow and splatter about in the mud. This makes little difference to their appearance, as they still sport the deep, dirty grey of the proverbial ugly duckling. I am delighted, and not a little surprised, that the five have all survived, given the dangers they face. The parents have obviously done a good job guarding their precious offspring.

Autumn is beginning to show its face around the parish, like an unwelcome intruder getting ever more confident as each day passes. Mornings are cooler now, and sometimes quite misty, with the plaintive autumn song of robins flowing through the quiet. Evenings see little flocks of starlings passing overhead, occasionally stopping off to land on our roof, where they cause consternation among the resident sparrows.

Another sign of autumn: a small cluster of creamy objects on the otherwise green lawn. Three fungi: four or five inches tall, with long, slender stems and jagged-edged flat caps. On closer inspection I can see the subtlety of their colour: the cream cap is splattered with brown, shading more intensely towards the shallow dip in the centre, while beneath the cap the gills are yellowish-buff, and pleasingly soft to the touch. I sniff one, and get the whiff of a delicate mushroomy smell not very different from the shop-bought version. But given my lack of fungal expertise, I decide that prudence is the better part of valour, and I am not tempted to take a bite.

Families of goldfinches, the youngsters lacking the adults' red faces, gather on the heads of thistles to feed, while swallows and house martins perch on the telegraph lines around the village centre, as if taking an inventory of their numbers before they depart. I shall miss them when they go.

On a clear night, at the start of the August bank holiday weekend, a full, round moon reflected in the long, straight rhyne turns oval in shape. This is caused by the unseen movements of small aquatic creatures just beneath the surface, making the waters ripple, and distorting the heavenly body above.

SEPTEMBER

SEPTEMBER OPENS WITH a cool, bright, misty morning. The dampness in the air is palpable in the hour after dawn, but soon burns off as the sun strengthens in the early-autumn sky. Phalanxes of swallows rise high in the air, the juvenile birds, with their short, stubby tails, testing their wings. I watch each day as they venture higher and higher, until they seem to reach the vapour trails of departed aircraft, growing fuzzy in the blue. From this aerial vantage point, the swallows can see into the next parish, and perhaps beyond, to Glastonbury Tor. But they cannot imagine what awaits them when they finally leave us, and the globe begins to unfold beneath their wings as they head south to Africa.

A pair of larger, darker birds passes swiftly overhead. From directly beneath, the falcons' streamlined, swept-back wings, dark helmets and streaked underparts mark them out as something special. They are hobbies: a sleek sports car to the kestrel's family hatchback. Like the swallows, these are young birds, not only testing out their flying skills, but their hunting abilities too. But this time, at least, the swallows are too quick for them, and they move on, their sleek arrow-shapes passing rapidly out of sight.

Soon afterwards, an adult hobby flies low overhead, seeking the benefit of surprise to nab a young swallow. But the parent birds are well aware of the danger, and pursue the falcon relentlessly. They take turns to peck at its back and tail with their sharp bills, until it is driven away, their urgent twitters of alarm echoing in its wake. It's easy to assume that predators have the upper hand in any encounter with their prey; but these attacks fail more often than not. And at some point the hobby must make a kill; for it, too, has a long journey ahead, all the way to the wide open savannah of the Zambezi River basin. There it will spend our winter hawking for insects – and the occasional swallow – before returning to the skies of Somerset next April.

It is still cool at this early hour, and steam is rising from my neighbour's compost heap. But one band of insects, the dragonflies, are already out and about, hunting their own prey with an equally ruthless efficiency. Ironically, dragonflies are often taken by hobbies, which have developed the ability to pursue this fast and furious insect, grabbing them in mid-air with their claws, before dispatching them with their hooked beak.

But today, the migrant hawker dragonflies are the predators, not the prey. They patrol just above the tops of the bushes and trees, dinking left, right, up, down, and sideways, on their wonderfully manoeuvrable wings, and grabbing any passing insect from a fly to a bumblebee with those fearsome jaws. Later in the day, as the sun warms the bramble bushes, I catch sight of one of these elegant creatures as it basks in the warm rays, its abdomen a delicate combination of brown, yellow and mauve. As its name suggests, the migrant hawker was once only a seasonal visitor to our shores. But in the past few years it has colonised southern and eastern Britain, and is now a familiar sight here in the parish during late summer and early autumn.

❀

NOW THAT SEPTEMBER is here, the nights are gradually drawing in. By 8 p.m. the sun has set, and the sky is almost dark. Outside the Old Vicarage, a hundred yards or so east of the village shop, a bird is perched on the telegraph wires: those same wires where, a few months ago, the first swallow of the summer was sitting.

The bird is a tawny owl. It sits on the topmost wire, unnoticed by drivers passing beneath on their journey home from work. Occasionally it twists its head slowly from side to side; though even when a medium-sized bat passes close by it takes no notice. After a few minutes, it drops off the wire on soft, silent wings, disappearing into the dense foliage of a nearby sycamore. In an hour or so, when the remaining glimmer of light has finally been enveloped by darkness, it will go hunting, listening for the rustling of hidden rodents below.

Here in the village, tawny owls are not uncommon; yet, given our many regular breeding birds, this is the one we see least often. We hear them though, as they call to each other, famously chronicled by Shakespeare in *Love's Labour's Lost*:

Then nightly sings the staring owl
Tu-whoo!
Tu-whit, tu-whoo! A merry note!

Shakespeare, who was usually pretty accurate in his bird references, makes an elementary mistake here. For this sound is not made by a single owl, but by a pair, performing in tandem. Thus the female calls 'kee-wick', while the male utters the more familiar, hooting call.

From early autumn onwards, I hear the hooting male more than any other time of year. This is a signal that the youngsters, born the previous spring, are now trying to establish their own territories for the breeding season to come. Because tawny owls like their own patch of ground – they rarely stray more than a few hundred yards from where they were born – the parent birds are forced to defend their little patch of land against their own offspring. This explains the increase in hooting on cold autumn nights.

And even, on occasion, during the day. Two or three times every autumn, at about eleven o'clock in the morning, I hear a tawny owl hooting from the garden next door. The first time I thought my ears were playing tricks on me. But so strong is the impulse to defend its territory against incomers that our neighbourhood male does indeed hoot during daylight hours.

During the autumn and winter, I sometimes come across a tawny owl at its daytime roost. These are never easy to find: an owl is surprisingly well camouflaged, despite its size, and can sit motionless in a hollow of a tree for hours on end, hidden to the world. Hidden, that is, until discovered by a curious passing bird. Then the unfortunate owl will find itself hassled from all sides, as the smaller birds join forces to see off this unwelcome predator. Usually the owl will tolerate the intruders until they back off, but if the harassment gets too much, it will be forced to move on and seek alternative daytime accommodation.

But they never go far: unlike the swallows, currently massing in the skies above the village shop, the tawny owl next door will never even see the next village, let alone Africa.

❁

THE NEXT MORNING, a sheet of mist hangs low over the distant Mendip Hills, as an unseen buzzard mews in the far distance, towards Chapel Allerton. Thick, heavy dew soaks the grass, the hedgerows and my feet, and I notice another sign of autumn: the teasels that only a few weeks ago were a delicate greenish-purple are now a rich, warm chestnut-brown. The willowherb has gone to seed too: fluffy balls of grey fur where once there were purplish-pink flowers.

Tall clumps of hogweed, hollow ghosts of their former glory, still stand along the lanes and droves, while splashes of orange in the hedgerows signal the ripening of rose-hips. I remember that we used to mark the start of the new school year by collecting rose-hips, crushing them, and removing the yellowish pulp containing the tiny seeds. Placed down the back of a classmate's shirt, they were remarkably effective as itching powder.

Just when I thought I had seen all the varying shades of purple, comes another: clumps of sloe berries studding the blackthorn bushes. One of Dylan Thomas's best-known lines, from the opening of *Under Milk Wood*, refers to this autumnal fruit: 'the sloe black, slow, black, crowblack, fishingboatbobbing sea'. The pun reveals the Welsh bard's preference for wordplay over accuracy: for sloes are never truly black. After the delicate pinkish-purples of the summer hedgerow flowers, this is a rich, deep, bluish-purple, more suited to autumn. In the early-morning air, each sloe has a whitish patina upon its surface. When rubbed gently between forefinger and thumb this disappears like the morning mist, revealing the smooth, grape-like fruit beneath.

Later in the year we harvest this purple bounty to make that time-honoured country beverage: sloe gin. There are almost as many recipes for this drink as there are black-thorn bushes: some people swear by picking the sloes after the first frost, while others simply pop them in the freezer for a day or two. They must then be pricked – either with a skewer or, traditionally, using a thorn from the black-thorn bush itself – before being doused with half a bottle of gin and a healthy serving of caster sugar. The resulting mixture is shaken up, then left forgotten on the kitchen windowsill until the following spring.

When the fluffy white flowers of the blackthorn come back into bloom, sometime in March, it reminds me to sample the result of last year's labours. I prefer it over crushed ice, as a post-prandial *digestif*; others swear by it neat. But however it is taken, the bitter-sweet, almost medicinal flavour of the sloes is a pleasant reminder of bright autumn days spent gathering the hard, purple fruit.

❀

THE INEXORABLE REDUCTION in day-length is having a profound effect on one village visitor. On the telegraph wires across Kingsway, a hundred or more swallows are gathering, responding to chemical changes in their brains which signal that it will soon be time to depart. From time to time, in response to some unseen alarm – false or otherwise – they all take to the air at once. Launching themselves off the wires, they plunge down towards the surface of the road before pulling steeply up, high into the sky; then scattering in loose, untidy flocks, their urgent twittering filling the cool air. Gradually, as the minutes pass and no danger appears, they calm down; gathering on the tops of the tall poplar trees by Lower Plaish Farm, before finally returning to their original perch.

During the whole performance, a pair of collared

doves has stayed put on the adjacent wire, watching the scenario unfold with the bored nonchalance we associate with this familiar garden bird. Yet collared doves have a story to tell which rivals that of the swallows. During the middle decades of the twentieth century they spread inexorably westwards across Europe like some conquering army, finally crossing the North Sea in the mid-1950s. This small, pinkish-brown dove – a bird we now so take for granted we barely notice its presence – had never even been seen in Britain when many of the older villagers were growing up.

And now, having arrived in rural Somerset, and made their home here, our collared doves show absolutely no inclination to travel any further. For them, this village has everything they need: food, water and plenty of places to nest. Let the swallows be consumed by their migratory restlessness; the doves are content to remain British citizens all year round.

❀

THE FIRST MIGRANTS to leave the village have already departed, taking advantage of a clear, moonlit night to do so. The dozens of reed warblers and handful of sedge warblers, whose songs were a constant chorus throughout May and June, first fell silent, then began to feed frantically on tiny aphids, almost doubling their weight. Finally they moulted in preparation for their journey, and headed off, under cover of darkness. For many, this is a leap into the dark in more ways than one: the offspring of those singing birds have never made the journey before and, if they are unlucky, may never get the chance to do so again.

After crossing the Channel they will head south through France and Spain, hopping across the Mediterranean via the Straits of Gibraltar to avoid a hazardous sea crossing, then skirting the borders of the Sahara, ending up in Western or Central Africa. They travel by night, unseen by human eyes and, more importantly, unseen by predators. Flying at night also enables them to avoid overheating, as the air is cooler.

September is the peak month for autumn migration, though it may begin as early as July and go on well into November. But September is undoubtedly the high point of the single greatest mass movement on earth. Close to 5 billion birds, of more than 200 different species, leave their breeding grounds across Europe and Asia and head south, the vast majority of them ending up in sub-Saharan Africa.

This was such a mystery to our ancestors that many – including such experienced observers as Gilbert White – struggled to accept that it was possible, instead believing that the birds hibernated under the surface of ponds and lakes. With hindsight it is easy to mock their ignorance, but the truth about these birds' journeys is hardly more believable. That a creature as small and delicate as a swallow can travel all the way to the southern tip of Africa and back – a return journey of over 10,000 miles – does appear to defy logic.

Nowadays we have solved many of the mysteries of migration, and know that these birds find their way using a combination of the earth's magnetic field, the sun, moon and stars, along with visible landmarks such as rivers and mountain ranges. But this knowledge doesn't stop us marvelling at the epic journeys these tiny birds take.

In spring, their arrival is fanfared by a burst of unfamiliar song, followed by the welcome sight of the birds themselves, but in autumn they make a quiet departure with no signal. Our wildlife, our parish and our country-side are diminished as a result.

❀

SOMETIME DURING THE middle of the month, the first true autumn morning dawns over the parish. The air holds a new and unfamiliar chill, and early risers have the unaccustomed experience of seeing steam on their breath as they stroll down to pick up the day's provisions at the village shop. A soft, low mist hangs over the fields, and the rhynes are giving off gouts of steam, obscuring the moorhens as they float along the still, glassy waters.

Habits are changing for people as well as wildlife. Winter clothes are being dug out from bottom drawers, central heating systems are bursting into life, and the children are back at school. And as if to remind us that the holiday season is well and truly over, some unseen hand has finally fixed the church clock, which proudly proclaims the time: five past seven.

Nature has risen earlier than us, as always, and our garden is thronged with neat, fresh-looking birds, showing off their spanking-new plumage after the summer moult. A pair of blackcaps has taken up territory on one of our elder bushes, and the male flits around, greedily feasting on the purple berries. From time to time his more timid, tan-capped mate pokes her head out too.

Along the damp, bumpy bridleway crossing Mark Moor, the last few clumps of daisies and red clover are wilting in the cool morning air. A robin calls loudly from a hawthorn hedge; and above it, on the topmost sprig, perches a plump, buffish-orange bird: a wheatear. This is unfamiliar territory: the closest place where wheatears breed is Exmoor or Salisbury Plain, though this bird could have come from as far afield as Scandinavia.

The wheatear may be the robin's cousin, but there is little love lost between them. Having established his autumn territory along this hedgerow, the robin is not prepared to tolerate any intruder, however far it might have travelled. So when the wheatear flies down onto the stony track the robin follows, uttering a peevish warning call, in an attempt to see off the newcomer. But the wheatear takes no notice, running in short bursts along the track on long, rangy legs, and occasionally stopping to pick up a morsel of insect food, before flying up to another perch.

As I get closer, the bird's fresh plumage and confiding nature suggest that this is a juvenile, probably only three or four months old. I appreciate the subtle pale, yellowish-buff of its belly shading darker on the upper breast, the jet-black tail, and as it flies a few yards along the path, the snow-white rump which gives the bird its name. For 'wheatear' has absolutely nothing to do with ears of wheat, but derives instead from an Anglo-Saxon word meaning 'white arse'.

The fresh, clear weather has brought other migrants out too. In the sky above Coombes Cider Mill a small, compact, solitary bird is heading resolutely south. Pale below, it briefly turns to reveal brownish upperparts: a sand martin. Like the wheatear, sand martins do not breed in the parish, but do regularly fly through in spring and autumn. Unlike the wheatear, sand martins travel by day, enabling them to feed on flying insects en route.

Occasionally, on clear, bright days in September, one or two much larger day-flying migrants may pass through the skies above the parish. Although most of our birds of prey are resident, a few do migrate, among them the osprey and the marsh harrier. Both have enjoyed consider-able rises in their fortunes over the past few decades, so are seen more often on their travels than they once were. Even so, encountering them is still a memorable experience.

I have seen each of these large raptors just once here, as they headed south. The osprey was flying high over my home, attracting the attention of the local ravens, which mobbed it unmercifully as it struggled through on long, flappy wings. The marsh harrier – a female, whose creamy cap contrasted with her chocolate-brown plumage – was far more determined. She flew low over the ground, head down like a racing cyclist, powering through the air on long, strong wings. In less than a minute she was gone.

✤

ON A CHILLY autumn evening, I head a few miles north of the parish, to the base of Cheddar Gorge. I wait by the River Yeo, which runs through the centre of this famous tourist town. I am looking for a scarce wild creature, and one that has declined more rapidly during my lifetime than any other British mammal: the water vole.

The river here has been dammed, the weir creating a narrow, fast-flowing stream, complete with mossy rocks and clumps of watercress; a Thatcher's cider bottle floats incongruously near the water's edge. The stream is crossed by a small stone bridge, with a steady flow of passers-by, but there is no sign of my rodent quarry. I am told they are very tame: and with so many people walking past, they must be.

Two grey wagtails are feeding along the river, perching on the rocks and flitting acrobatically up into the air to catch tiny midges. As I wait a sparrowhawk passes overhead, its unmistakable flapping and gliding flight causing a momentary panic among the local songbirds.

The sparrowhawk aside, this is a good place to spend the winter, being a degree or two warmer than the surrounding countryside. The river's flow prevents ice-ups in all but the harshest winters, and provides a constant source of tiny insects all season long.

I become mesmerised by the movement of the river, as the slow, inky-black water picks up speed over the rocks, its constant movement creating the illusion of stasis. The wagtails flit from one rock to another, constantly moving their tails to keep balance, but there is still no sign of any water voles. Eventually, as dusk begins to fall, I give up my vigil and return home.

As the autumn equinox passes, and we begin the long, slow slide towards winter, my quest to see the water voles of Cheddar seems doomed to failure. Then I get a tip-off. My wife Suzanne has begun work at the local medical centre, and one day she notices a movement in the river alongside the car park. It may be a rat, it may even be a fish; but I decide it's worth another visit.

So one afternoon I return to Cheddar and walk carefully along the river, peering through the foliage of the bankside trees while trying to stop my children falling in. As soon as I get within sight of the bright, clear water I catch sight of a rapid movement beneath the surface. Unfortunately it is not a rodent, but a fast-moving fish.

Just as I am about to leave, though, a real surprise; a thrush-sized bird hops up on the rocks by the weir: a dipper. For a brief moment I get the classic view of this wonderful waterbird as it bobs up and down on springy legs, before zipping off into the distance like a giant wren.

Dippers are generally found on upland rivers and streams, where fast-flowing water provides enough oxygen for the aquatic insects on which they feed. They catch these by submerging themselves beneath the surface of the water, then walking along the riverbed like an avian submarine. It may seem incongruous to find dippers in this urban setting, but I shouldn't be surprised: the River Yeo, flowing straight down off the Mendips, provides the perfect habitat for this, our only aquatic songbird. And in my excitement in seeing the dipper, I momentarily forget that my original quest, to see the water voles, remains unfulfilled.

❊

THE NIGHTS ARE lengthening, the days are getting cooler, and the butterflies in our garden are having their final fling. With fallen fruits littering the lawn, a troupe of red admirals has arrived to make the most of this bumper harvest. One sunny morning, as I am hanging out the washing, at least half a dozen of these gaudy insects appear. Just hatched, and box-fresh in appearance, they are feasting on a glut of apples, pears and plums.

Drinking this half-rotten fruit has a strange side effect: the butterflies become intoxicated by the products of fermentation. This means I can get so close to them that

I need to take out my reading glasses to focus. Only then can I truly appreciate their stunning colours, a delicate and perfectly symmetrical pattern of black and orange-red, set off by the snow-white patches towards the tips of their wings.

Can there be a more beautiful British butterfly? I'm hard pushed to think of one, and wonder if this were a rarity, like the swallowtail or one of the fritillaries, people might rate it more highly than they do. As it is, we usually notice the first one of the year, and the rest of the time we ignore them, instead of stopping to admire their gorgeous patterns and colours.

Like those invading painted ladies, red admirals are migrants, coming to our shores from continental Europe each spring. Once here they gradually spread north throughout Britain, some reaching as far as Shetland. After laying their eggs on the upper surface of stinging nettles, they then die, so the ones I am seeing in my garden at this time of year are the newly hatched offspring of those long-distance travellers.

In a month or so, as the cold weather really takes hold, these splendid butterflies will head off to find the last flowers of the year, ivy blossom. They will eke out a last few precious drops of nectar while basking in the rays of the weak late-autumn sunshine. Most will then die, but in the past few years some red admirals have begun to over-winter in southern England, hibernating in garden sheds before emerging on sunny days in the New Year. I remind myself to remember to look for these sleeping beauties, come November.

❦

AS THE MONTH draws to a close, a bright, sunny day marks summer's final fling. Common darter dragonflies mate frantically on the warm concrete paths in our garden, each male grabbing the female in a tight embrace before curling his abdomen around to meet hers, in a brief but passionate act of congress. A flush of tall daisies, their white petals tinged purple in the morning sun, attract honeybees, each desperately loading up on nectar before returning to their distant hives. And overhead, against the cloud-flecked sky, the occasional swallow continues to head south, on its intrepid journey to Africa.

OCTOBER

A MILD AND BLUSTERY day at the beginning of the month, as a hundred or so villagers gather in the parish church for the annual Harvest Festival. Predictably, but comfortingly, the service opens with that rousing Victorian hymn, 'We Plough the Fields and Scatter'. Swelled by the voices of the village schoolchildren, and coinciding with the first weak rays of sun shining in through the east window, the chorus is suitably uplifting. The words of the hymn seem curiously apt, for this year the weather has gone back to something approaching normal; with snow in winter, summer warmth and sunshine to swell the grain, autumn breezes and, today at least, soft refreshing rain.

After the service is over, and the rain has stopped, we take a family walk down the lane behind our home in search of our own share of seasonal fruitfulness: blackberries. In the traditional calendar of natural events, we are only just in time. Old Michaelmas Day on 11 October is, according to folklore, the time the devil spits on blackberries, making them inedible. A tasting of the current crop confirms that the blackberries may be small, but they are still sweet and tasty.

When I was a child, blackberry-picking was an annual event. From midsummer to early autumn we would take every chance we could to grab handfuls of the dark, squishy fruit; usually eating far more than we ever took home. Nowadays, I suspect the fear of consuming anything that hasn't been processed, packaged and purchased stops many people from taking advantage of this abundant food supply. Down the road at the Highbridge branch of Asda, blackberries are on special offer, marked down to £1.99 a punnet. Yet in the lanes around the parish you can collect a basketful for free in a few minutes, though hardly anyone does. The vast majority of the local blackberries go unpicked and uneaten, left instead for the birds.

But picking blackberries is more than simply an enjoyable diversion on a country walk. In an age when we have lost the connection between what we eat and the land where our food comes from, this autumnal activity offers a tangible link to our foraging past. Not all that long ago – certainly in our grandparents' time – this hedgerow bounty was a welcome addition to a poor and often monotonous diet. It was also a major crop here on the levels, with the fruit used for dyes and to make jam; the income this generated bought the village children boots and shoes for the winter.

Picking blackberries is also hard enough work to make you feel you have earned the right to eat your harvest. Those annoying prickles, which help protect the fruit from being taken, require a degree of care if you want to avoid being scratched. We return home with hands stained mauve by blackberry juice, along with a few red marks as a sign of the sacrifice we made to pick them. That evening, we enjoy a pie made from home-grown cooking apples and the fruits of our blackberrying labours; a fitting end to the day when we stood in church to give thanks for the food we eat.

❁

As we enter the last quarter of the year, so the creatures of the parish begin to enter our home. House invasions are a perennial feature of life in the country, especially in an old farmhouse like ours, here since the middle of the eighteenth century. In spring and early summer we play host to baby birds; mainly fledgling sparrows or robins which have tumbled out of their nest, and wandered through our permanently open back door. They are occasionally joined by a jackdaw in the chimney: either an adult building a nest, or a clumsy juvenile which has lost its footing.

Toads are another annual visitor, especially when we get a spell of rainy weather, which encourages them to venture away from the safety of their hiding places. The lack of a doorstep enables them to crawl doggedly inside, where they sit on the wooden floor looking rather lost, before we pick them up and release them into a damp corner of our garden.

Moths, of course, are a regular sight on summer mornings, as we usually leave the bathroom light on in case the children get up during the night. Large yellow underwings are the most frequent visitors, blundering around in the shower or lurking behind the net curtains before fluttering out to scare the unwary. But smaller moths venture indoors too, including on one occasion a species I hadn't seen before, a snout: a triangular-shaped moth with hooked wingtips, and the peculiar proboscis that gives this insect its name.

But these are just the forerunners of the true invasion, which takes place now in early autumn. Craneflies – daddy-long-legs to every new generation of children – dance around on their six springy legs as they seek to escape from the human inhabitants of our home. They superficially resemble spiders, and indeed one of the autumn spiders we see most often is, rather confusingly, named the 'daddy-long-legs spider'. This spindly creature hides away in the cooler parts of the house, so that from October onwards our younger children are wary of entering the downstairs toilet. When I see this spider tucked inside its rather pathetic web in the angle between wall and ceiling, it's hard to resist poking it gently with the end of a pencil. In response, it bounces back and forth too rapidly for my eye to see anything but a blur; a useful defence mechanism to foil predators.

Daddy-long-legs spiders may look weedy and insignificant, but they have given rise to a popular urban myth. It is said that this harmless-looking creature contains a venom so potent that, were its jaws powerful enough to pierce human skin, it would kill you instantly. Helped by the Internet, this 'fact' is now well and truly embedded in the public consciousness, and the rather dull truth is unable to compete. The venom of the daddy-long-legs spider is actually rather weaker than that of most other spiders, and can do us no harm.

Two larger spiders – the huge and hairy (and to many people terrifying) *Tegenaria domestica* and *Tegenaria gigantea* – also emerge at this time of year, scuttling across sitting-room carpets to hysterical screams up and down the land. The ones we see are usually males, on the lookout for a mate; if you think these look big, you should see the females. Fortunately, after a few weeks these love-lorn arachnids have found each other and settled down out of sight, to breed.

Outside, in the parks and playgrounds around the parish, it's the local children's favourite time of year. The leaves of the horse-chestnut trees are turning an orangey-brown, and beneath every one is a treasure trove of spiky green balls, each beginning to split open to reveal the dark, shiny fruit within. Is there any natural object as instantly alluring as the conker? Nothing else has quite the same appeal, and even now, more than forty years after I picked one up as a small child, I still get the same thrill each year when I find the first polished conker of the season.

In the playground by Blackford Church, where back in chilly February I saw the first catkins of spring, there are dozens of conkers. I have a vision of the local children collecting them as I once did; taking them home by the pocketful, and patiently drilling a neat hole through each one before threading it onto a piece of string in readiness for combat. For this, of course, has always been the enduring appeal of conkers, especially for generations of small boys. The fact that this bountiful fruit doesn't just look good but can be used in the famous playground game, simply adds to its appeal.

The current obsession with health and safety has led to the game of conkers being banned in some schools; but I thought the practice might still survive here, in these rural surroundings. Judging by the number of unclaimed beauties lying here beneath the swings and the see-saw, perhaps it doesn't.

❈

IN MOST AUTUMNS we enjoy a classic 'Indian summer'. Temperatures still plummet by night, and mornings dawn cool, with clear blue skies. But as the day progresses, in sheltered parts of the parish at least, a southerly breeze and the soft warmth of the sun belie the lateness of the season. Some days, the only reason we know it's not May or June is the absence of swallows twittering in the skies above.

Their place is taken by starlings, whose high-pitched whistles have a less melodic, more metallic quality than the swallows – almost a mechanical timbre at times. As the air warms up in the early afternoon, little flocks of starlings fly up above the village gardens, spreading out from their usual tight formation, and grazing on insects floating in the air. They display an unusual grace – not a word we usually associate with these chunky little birds – as they stretch out their bills to grab their invisible prey.

I mow the lawn for what I hope will be the last time this autumn; though in some years another cut is required in November, or even December. Instead of the grass moths of spring and summer, long-legged craneflies leap from beneath the mower's blades, bouncing away in search of an uncut patch of sward where they can hide from predators.

Despite the warmth, signs of autumn are more and more visible; not least in the absence of those pink and purple flowers that lined the rhynes and hedgerows during the past few months. Purple loosestrife, which only a few weeks ago was still flowering in any damp corner, has gone to seed, while only a few sad, drooping fronds of willow-herb remain. Clouds of midges still hang in the air in more sheltered areas; but within a week or so I shall hear the high-pitched call of returning redwings in the night sky; and soon afterwards feel the crunch of early-morning frosts beneath my boots.

❀

ON A COOL, bright morning, towards the end of this Indian summer, weather patterns are beginning to shift into autumn. But the sun is still shining along Kingsway as I return home after taking my children to school. Driving is never the best way to notice wildlife, as the windscreen and engine noise cut us off from the subtle signs that alert us to the presence of something unusual: birdsong, the buzz of an insect, or the distant flick of a wing.

But I can hardly fail to notice the flock of birds flying low over the rhyne beside the road. Just as when you catch sight of an old friend, when you least expect to see them, my brain does a double take. Not starlings, as I first thought, but swallows: more than sixty of them, feeding frantically on the few tiny insects that still remain airborne. In the bright morning light they swerve expertly from side to side, using their tails as brakes, and keeping to the area directly above the water, where the flies, gnats and midges are most concentrated.

It is almost a month since the village swallows left their perch on the telegraph wires for the last time, and headed away into the blue. I have long since grown used to their absence; yet now, in the middle of October, here they are again. Not the same birds, of course: our swallows are way to the south by now, flying over the Mediterranean or crossing the Sahara.

Given the run of north-easterly winds, I suspect this little group of swallows, with a solitary house martin in tow, have come from Scandinavia. Having flown across the North Sea they are now making their way through Britain, finding food wherever they can, before heading out over the English Channel on the next leg of their journey. After feeding they rest for a while on the telegraph wires, reminding me, as they always do, of musical notes on a set of staves. As they perch they hold out their wings, expertly preening their feathers with their stubby bills to keep them in tip-top condition, and to remove parasites (though some mites and ticks are so persistent they accompany the birds all the way to Africa and back). From time to time each bird will swoop down off the wire to feed, before returning to its original perch.

In one of his early poems, John Clare wrote of seeing two swallows hawking for insects in late October, and how he wished they could stay for the whole of the winter:

> *For in the unsocial weather ye would fling*
> *Gleanings of comfort through the winter wide*
> *Twittering as wont above the old fireside*
> *And cheat the surly winter into spring.*

Some swallows stay even later: a couple of years ago, on a wet and windy day in early December, my neighbour Mick telephoned me to report a single swallow flying around the field next to his allotment, just across the road from my home. I must admit I was sceptical, until he showed me a brief snatch of video footage he had taken of the bird. It was, indeed, a swallow; though sadly I doubt if it ever made it all the way to Africa.

I look up, and the swallows have already gone: refuelled, restocked and refreshed. I say a silent goodbye. This may seem self-indulgent, but given that these birds are so much a part of my life, and the life of my fellow villagers, I shall miss them; until they return to visit us once again, half a year from now.

❀

A CHILLY DAWN; not quite the first frost, although one is forecast for tomorrow night. Now, at half past six in the morning, the skies are totally clear, the stars of the Plough and Orion's Belt still shine directly above the village, and the eastern sky is beginning to glow a dull shade of red. A sense of anticipation is in the air, too; for we are going bird-ringing.

Last night I spent an hour fumbling around in the darkness setting up three mist-nets, with my friend and fellow-birder Ed, a qualified bird-ringer. First brought to Britain from Japan back in the 1950s, mist-nets are a truly amazing piece of equipment. Stretched between two sturdy metal poles, they allow us to catch a bird without harming it. The unsuspecting creature simply flies into the ultra-fine net, drops down into a pouch below, and waits there calmly until the ringer extracts it; a process which Ed carries out with considerable skill and care.

By seven o'clock dawn has broken, the stars are rapidly fading in the sky, and a wren is singing his unseasonal song in the blackthorn and cider-apple hedgerow along the western side of the garden. As well as the morning chill I feel a frisson of anticipation: will we catch any birds, or will our nets remain empty?

But we immediately score a bullseye, in the shape of two wrens, one rather more crotchety than his companion. Ed carefully removes these 'flying mice', as he calls them, expertly untangling their long claws and slipping each bird head first into its own small, cotton bag. We return to the back of his car where he has set up an impromptu ringing station. Each bird is weighed and measured, revealing that one wren is slightly larger than its companion, weighing in at over a third of an ounce.

Then, most importantly, a tiny metal ring is placed around its leg, before being squeezed gently shut with a pair of special pliers. My colleague Ruth dutifully notes down the statistics, which are sent to the British Trust for Ornithology for analysis and safe keeping. So even if the bird is never found again, the data obtained by catching it will be invaluable in extending our knowledge about our birds.

The children have roused themselves from their beds to watch, so rapt with attention they don't appear to be feeling the morning cold. Subsequent net rounds produce a final total of seventeen birds from ten different species, ranging in size from a young male blackbird, weighing almost 100 grams to a tiny goldcrest, which at just 5 grams is exactly half the weight of the larger of the two wrens. We also catch seven goldfinches, as well as a single chiffchaff, house sparrow, blue tit, great tit, dunnock and robin. Each of the children gets the chance to release a bird; cradling its soft body in their cupped hands, before slowly opening them and watching as it regains its freedom. It is an experience I hope they never forget.

We speculate on how far these little birds have come. Although the majority are likely to have hatched out nearby, perhaps even in the garden itself, others could have travelled much further. Even the tiny goldcrest might have flown all the way across the North Sea. If he has, he is not the only one to have come so far. This morning, as we unfurled the nets for the first time, a high-pitched 'seep' from the sky above signalled the very first redwing of the autumn. It had flown here from Iceland or Scandinavia, and was passing over the parish on its way south, possibly to France. Later on, we saw the very last swallows of the year heading over the field behind Mill Batch. For the first time I can recall, I have witnessed these summer visitors leaving on the same day as the first birds of winter arrive.

❀

AS THE WEATHER turns colder, and the vegetation begins its long, slow retreat towards winter, so the wildlife of the parish becomes easier to see. This is partly due to necessity, as the lower temperatures and shorter days mean they must forage for food in a more concentrated timespan. The days of lazing around out of sight are over; time is now precious, and we human observers are reaping the benefit.

So one morning I get my best-ever view of a stoat – a ruthlessly effective mammalian predator. The sighting comes as I approach at thirty miles per hour, in the comfort of my car, rather than on my usual mode of transport, the bicycle. With stoats, all I usually see is a black-tipped tail vanishing into the long grass; or, on one memorable occasion, the momentary glimpse of the whole animal, frozen in mid-air, as it dived for cover. Today, though, this animal is far more cooperative, and I am able to watch it through binoculars (and a rather grubby windscreen) for upwards of a minute, which, when you are talking about this particular creature, feels like an age.

I take in its sheer splendour: the long and bushy tail; the chestnut-brown head, face and upperparts; small, rounded ears; and, most striking of all as it lollops along the edge of the roadside towards me, the soft, creamy-yellow underparts, extending from just beneath its chin to its belly. I hold my breath as it approaches; and then, aware that it is being watched, it returns to form and zips into the grass beneath the hedgerow, never to reappear.

❈

ONE COLD EVENING I don my quilted jacket, gloves and hat, and cycle over to Rick and Heather's home in Harp Road. Both come from well-known local farming families, and both have lived in the village all their lives; Rick still farms the fields and yard next to my home, shearing his sheep or holding his cattle in the pens there.

We discuss the many changes since his childhood, in the decades after the Second World War. His own father, Reg, started with almost nothing – just a handful of dairy cattle he took when he left his mother and step-father's farm at the age of sixteen. He and Rick's mother worked hard to build up a successful business, growing and selling anything they could, so Rick and his sisters were enlisted as extra farmhands from an early age. He recalls hoeing the hard earth to grow swedes as winter food for the cattle; and how his father used to ride home on his bike, a milk pail balanced with one arm on his head.

In those days the majority of the farms around the village were home to a herd of dairy cattle. But the drop in the farm-gate price for milk, together with golden handshakes for getting out of milk production, eventually sounded the death knell for the local dairy industry. Today, of the fifteen or so working farms in the parish, only a handful produce milk. One of these, Perry Farm, is right behind our home; so we can still see the cows being taken to and from their pasture, every morning and evening.

Rick has seen many changes in the wildlife of the parish. Hares were once common; while buzzards – indeed any bird of prey apart from the kestrel – were a very unusual sight up to about ten years ago. House sparrows are still here in small flocks, but in those days they thronged the field over the road in their thousands, feeding on barley and flying up into the hedgerow when anyone came within sight.

On my ride home, I head along the back route of Northwick Road, which has been converted from a muddy drove into a tarmac lane within Rick's and Heather's life-times. Along the way I hear a curious sound, rather like a cross between a barking dog and the cry of the lapwing. It is a little owl, calling in the darkness, out of sight. I do see this elusive bird in the parish from time to time, as it mainly hunts by day; but did not know there was a territory here until now.

My nocturnal surprises are not quite over. As I reach the main road through the centre of the village, a move-ment along the pavement catches my eye. It is a badger, loping along towards me utterly unaware of my presence; until the light westerly breeze wafts my scent towards him. He immediately stops, lifts his nose, sniffs, then dives away into an adjacent garden.

Before I left, Rick had presented me with a gift: two brace of partridge. These are the French or red-legged rather than the native English grey variety, which he shot down on the levels a day or two ago. I bring them home, tucked into my cycle pannier, before hanging them on a hook by our back door.

This presents me with a dilemma: not a moral but a purely practical one. Although I wouldn't choose to do it myself, I have no problem with my neighbours shooting game birds in season; provided that the birds are subsequently eaten. But as a townie by birth and upbringing, I have absolutely no clue how to pluck, draw and prepare a partridge.

Fortunately we have established a good relationship with our local butcher's in Wedmore; so I give Mike a quick ring. Plucking them will take too long, he tells me; but he will have them skinned and the guts removed by Tuesday if I can pop them over. Before I do, I take a closer look at the subtle shades of their plumage and admire the way that the blacks, greys and chestnuts seem to merge into one another. Their scarlet feet, with their outsized toes for running rapidly across uneven ground, hang limp and motionless beneath their lifeless bodies.

❀

ALONG THE SOUTHERN border of the parish, the River Brue meanders slowly but steadily westwards, passing through the hamlet of Bason Bridge, then beneath the M5 motorway. It skirts the town of Highbridge before, five miles or so from here, it finally reaches the sea. Well, not exactly the sea. The mouth of the Brue disgorges its waters into another, larger river, the Parrett, both then mingling with waters from the longest of all our rivers, the Severn, in Bridgwater Bay.

To reach the estuary I park in Clyce Road, named after the local word for a sluice gate. I cross a footbridge over the river, then a stile, and immediately the vista opens out from suburban sprawl into an open, windswept landscape.

It may be two hours after dawn, but a strong, full moon is still in the sky, while the autumn sun reflects a motley selection of pleasure boats in the water. As the river widens, the usual mallards and mute swans feed on the still, calm waters; while a touch of exotica is added by the presence of a little egret. No matter how often I see them, egrets always compel me to take a closer look. Wings bowed, neck hunched, legs trailing behind, this vision of pure white crosses over the river and seeks refuge in the reedbed on the far side.

The sound of distant herring gulls lends the scene a maritime air. But this is an illusion: the waters ahead of me are more river than sea, despite their breadth. One difference is the smell: Bridgwater Bay may look and sound like the sea, but it certainly doesn't have the tangy, salty scent of true coastline.

Nevertheless, the meeting of these three rivers, all of which are tidal here, does create the ideal habitat for many coastal birds. In the far distance, over the shingle promontory of Steart, I can already see clouds of waders flashing pale and dark in the morning light. Small flocks of lapwings and curlews have come inland to feed on low-lying grassy fields while the tide is at its full height, covering their feeding areas for an hour or two. The curlews probe delicately into the muddy earth with that impossibly long, downcurved bill. Then, flushed by a dog-walker and his beast, they rise up into the air and wheel back towards the coast, uttering the evocative whistling call that gives them their name.

Another high-pitched sound, and a flash of colour and movement catches my eye: that little jewel of a bird, the kingfisher. It flies up the river channel, and I wait for it to disappear as they usually do. But to my delight it turns and lands on a small mooring post by the bank, a hundred yards or so before the river's mouth, giving me a wonderful view.

To call a kingfisher 'blue' is to underrate both the colour and the bird; for it ranges through a dazzling palette of turquoise, green, electric-blue and indigo, depending on the angle at which the bird is facing, while the rusty orange underparts seem to reflect the sun itself. No doubt this bird will spend the winter here: their fishy diet makes kingfishers especially vulnerable to hard winters, but it can be sure that however harsh the weather becomes, these estuarine waters will not freeze over.

I pass through a modern, and rather unromantic, kissing gate; and a few yards further on, after one last meander, the Brue finally reaches its destination. The path bends southwards along the eastern side of the bay, parallel to the sea wall, and I stop to take in the scene before me: the Quantock Hills to my left, and the island of Steep Holm to the right.

Across the mouth of the River Parrett, vast flocks of waders are twisting and turning, moving like a single, protean organism. They flash black and white as they change direction in an instant, before returning to their high-tide roost on the shingle spit. Despite the chilly air, a thin layer of heat-haze forms ripples across the surface of the water; and this, combined with the movement of the birds, creates a bizarre optical effect.

As they come closer I can see that what I thought was one flock is, in fact, two: the smaller group being dunlins, and the larger, presumably, knots. It is liberating to be so far away that I can forget about looking at the detail of their plumage, and simply concentrate on their aesthetic qualities. As they loop, I relish the sheer pleasure of watching these birds, like vast shoals of fish, weaving complex patterns through the fresh morning air.

What better testimony than the scene in front of me, against the hare-brained, and fortunately now defunct, scheme to harness the tidal energy of the River Severn by building a massive barrage across its mouth. A barrage which, had it gone ahead, would have destroyed this unique habitat, and driven the birds away for ever.

Further along, on a rough patch of grass dotted with the odd pool of water, there are little flocks of starlings, meadow pipits and skylarks, all feeding on the damp, grassy area behind the sea wall. Accompanying them, to my surprise, is a rather late wheatear. This perky little bird bobs up and down on lichen-covered boulders, flicking its tail, and then running across the short, cropped grass. Tonight, if the skies remain clear, it will head off, southwards to Africa. The one I saw in the parish back in September will already be there.

The pipits keep up a constant calling: a light, thin, high-pitched 'sip'. From time to time the skylarks join in, with a burst of notes and even, occasionally, a snatch of full song. The sounds of autumn are much less varied than those of spring, but they have their own special charm, especially against the gentle lapping of waves over mud, as the tide begins to drop.

I turn for home. Thus ends my brief excursion beyond the western borders of the parish; to a place which, although utterly different in landscape and character, is umbilically connected by the River Brue to my home patch. The link between the village on the levels, and the open sea, may be well hidden, but it is still deep and true.

NOVEMBER

ALL SAINTS' DAY, at the beginning of November, often marks a dramatic change in the weather, as the last traces of summer finally fade, and the true character of autumn is revealed. Some years this is marked by hard frosts, but our unpredictable climate means that dank, wet weather is equally likely.

When Atlantic weather systems dominate, wave after wave of depressions sweep across that vast ocean, and funnel up the Bristol Channel, bringing more rain to an already sodden landscape. The ground soaks up the extra water for a while, but as the weeks go by the roads are awash with muddy puddles, while little pools begin to form on the fields. Day after day, the west wind whips across this flat, open land, battering the stunted trees and hedges into submission.

Just when the memory of the departed birds of summer is fading, the winter visitors start to arrive. Each night, the thin, high-pitched calls of redwings fall from the darkness like showers of autumn rain. They have come from Iceland and Scandinavia, where they breed in the low thickets of dwarf willow and birch alongside streams and bogs, or under the eaves of rural barns. I once saw a singing redwing in Iceland, and was struck by the blandness of its song; a less tuneful version of a thrush or blackbird, without the sweetness of either. But here, in their winter quarters, their only sound is this single, sibilant note.

By November redwings are here in force, thronging

the hedgerows of the parish. As cars pass by they scatter into the air like sparks blown from a bonfire; an appropriate image, for one of their local names is 'wind thrush'. Although they are often mistaken for starlings, there is something about their silhouette, with their blunter wings and plumper body, which marks them out as different. Only when they gather in the muddy fields to feed does their beauty reveal itself. Neater and darker than the song thrush, they show a rich, rusty-orange patch on their flanks, and a broad, creamy stripe running just above each eye.

Whenever I see redwings, their larger cousin the fieldfare is not usually far away. This is another striking and colourful bird, its deep chestnut back contrasting with a pale grey head, and creamy-yellow underparts marked with bold, black chevrons. Noticeably longer and bulkier than the redwing, this lanky thrush is another winter visitor here, crossing the North Sea from Scandinavia. As a child I recall seeing huge squadrons of fieldfares heading southwest over the flat north Norfolk landscape, uttering the harsh, chacking call which signals their annual appearance.

Fieldfares usually arrive a week or two later than redwings; perhaps their size means they can better withstand the cold, and stay put on their breeding grounds a little longer. But by mid-November they are everywhere: dotted across the fields, thronging the hedgerows, or simply proceeding high across the sky on their way further south. Those that do stay here certainly make their presence felt, with flocks of several hundred birds stripping a hedgerow bare, before moving on to fill their stomachs with another crop of berries.

The early arrivals also feed in the local cider-apple orchards, where loads of unpicked fruit litter the grass beneath the trees. Later in the season, if the winter stays mild, they will range across the wet fields, turning over clods of damp earth with their bills in search of worms and other invertebrate prey.

By late February many redwings and fieldfares have already started to head back north and east, and although a few linger on into early March, by the middle of the month they are gone. I miss their presence, and look forward to that night, the following autumn, when I shall hear that thin, high-pitched call of the redwing once again, in the darkened skies above the village.

❁

ON FIREWORK WEEKEND we experience a suitably explosive run of weather, starting with a badly timed downpour flooding out the Bonfire Night celebrations at the White Horse Inn. The following day dawns bright and warm, but during the night there is a heavy hailstorm. Next morning, little chunks of ice are still clustered on the ground like shattered glass from a car windscreen.

I am up on the Mendips, only a few miles north of the parish, but at least 600 feet higher in altitude. We gather in the car park of the Swan Inn at Rowberrow, several hours before opening time: a dozen eager disciples of wild-food enthusiast Adrian Boots. We are going on a fungal foray: to learn how to forage for free food, ideally without ending up in the local casualty department.

The landscape could hardly be more different from the flat, wet vistas I am used to. We are walking through a dense woodland: little stands of oak and beech surrounded by great swathes of Norway spruce; the fast-growing, economically profitable 'Christmas tree' we know so well. Wildlife is both thin on the ground and hard to see among the dense, inky foliage. The only evidence that anything is here at all is the occasional snatch of sound: the trill of a wren, the peeping of goldcrests and coal tits, or the harsh screech of a distant jay. Closed, claustrophobic, this is not a place in which I feel at ease.

Adrian is a cheerful, personable young man, given to dispensing useful nuggets of wisdom, such as 'the only rule of thumb about eating fungi is that there are no rules of thumb'. This is crucial advice, given the widespread belief that if a mushroom is white, grows in a field, has a flat cap or keeps a silver spoon bright when cooking, then it is safe to eat. Just one problem: several deadly poisonous mushrooms fit into one or more of these categories.

So all we can do is learn the key identification points of the edible and deadly varieties, and never trust to luck – a single moment of complacency may prove fatal. Later on, one of our party picks an innocent-looking stemmed mushroom with a greenish-brown cap, which Adrian identifies as a death-cap: a fungus that if we were tempted to cook and eat it, would prove fatal. Point made.

We spread out through the woods like a police forensic team, carefully scanning every inch of ground in front of us. Our task is made much more difficult by last night's bad weather: fungi are easily damaged, and a direct hit from a hailstone can make a deep dent on their soft surface. Even when we do find a specimen, there is evidence that something else has got here first: chunks missing, or tooth-marks along the edges, suggesting that it has been nibbled by a passing slug or small mammal. All in all, the fungi are not looking their best.

Walking through a wood at such a slow, deliberate pace changes the way you appreciate the landscape. I begin to notice the patterns of the fallen beech leaves arranged in a random collage, ranging from chocolate-brown, through chestnuts, to buffs, yellows and the occasional tinge of lime-green, the summer shade retained even at this late stage of the year. The veins of the leaves overlap each other to make abstract patterns, intermingling with the greens of the surrounding brambles, ferns and moss.

Many fungi are picked, but few are chosen; and as Adrian inspects our baskets he discards most of what we have found. The temptingly named honey fungus is, he tells us, often sold in markets as an edible variety. If you do eat it, you may get a nasty stomach upset, though it won't actually kill you. Coral fungus does indeed resemble bright orange corals – you wouldn't want to eat it, even if you could.

The edible varieties bear out Adrian's warning that appearance cannot be used as a guide to safe eating, as they could hardly be more different from one another. The common yellow brittlegill, chunky with a flat yellowish cap; the tiny amethyst deceiver, the colour of royal purple, its long, slender stalk topped with a cap the size of a penny; and several giant puffballs. These are not, alas, the huge football-sized mushrooms that can feed a family; but small, weedy specimens, whose softness to the touch indicates they have already begun to develop spores, so are no longer edible. We also find wood blewits and a beautiful orangey-yellow chanterelle, which when gently squeezed emits a delicate scent of ripe apricots.

The most peculiar specimen is Judas's ear, which does indeed resemble a shrivelled, rubbery version of a human ear. This particular fungus has a long history: it grows on elder, and got its name from the belief that, after he betrayed Christ, Judas Iscariot hanged himself from an elder tree. This is commemorated in both the scientific name for the fungus, *Auricularia auricula-judae*, and its old vernacular name, 'Jew's ear', which in these more sensitive times has understandably fallen into disuse. Another fungus rich in folklore, though not edible, is King Alfred's cakes – so called because when you cut open these little hard lumps they look as if they are burnt inside, a feature which would have reminded our ancestors of the famous royal cake-burning incident that took place a few miles south of here.

Just before lunchtime, we come across what looks like a cluster of bright red apples strewn across the forest floor. These are the fly agaric, whose name comes from its traditional use as an insecticide. However, its main claim to fame is that indigenous people across Siberia have historically used it for its hallucinogenic properties, as part of their shamanic traditions.

We decide against trying to recreate this ancient practice. Instead Adrian heats up his Primus stove, chops up the few edible fungi we have managed to gather, and sautés them in a mixture of butter and olive oil. After a long morning's walk through the woods, the smell of sizzling mushrooms is as intoxicating as any hallucinogen; and when we finally get to sample the spoils of our morning's work, the experience is little short of culinary bliss. Each tastes subtly different from the others, with a sweet, nutty flavour far more satisfying than shop-bought mushrooms. The texture, too, is different: more squishy than firm, but not unpleasant.

As we eat, Adrian tells us about the complex relationship between trees and fungi. Tree roots are not very good at obtaining nutrition, so they use networks of underground fungi to do it for them. What we see on the surface – the fruiting bodies we call mushrooms and toadstools – are but a tiny fraction of what lies out of sight, beneath the soil. The time and effort it has taken us to collect this meagre offering is a salutary reminder of just how tough life was for our hunter-gatherer ancestors; and how good they must have been at knowing exactly where to look, and what to pick. Better than me, anyway.

By late afternoon the light has turned soft and even as it percolates through the trees, and the smell of the woodland begins to intensify: a not unpleasant blend of dampness and decay. As we return to the warmth of the Swan Inn for a welcome pint, a solitary raven croaks unseen overhead; reminding us of the wilderness we have shared with nature for the past few hours.

❀

ON REMEMBRANCE SUNDAY, the Union flag lies limp and stiff against the flagpole on the village church, as a high-pressure system builds across southern Britain, and the first real frosts of autumn begin to bite.

Once again the landscape is transformed. Early in the mornings, as the mist rising from the rhynes begins to clear, the frost grips the grass like a white shroud. During the hour or so after sunrise, a bird we don't usually think of as a migrant heads purposefully across the parish skies. Large, powerful and pale against the clear blue sky in the early-morning light: flocks of wood pigeons are heading south in search of food.

While clearing out the attic in one of our outbuildings, I come across a bizarre, and at first puzzling, sight.

Hundreds of small, feathery objects, ranging in colour from deep brown, through buff, black, yellow and faded orange, litter the wooden floorboards. After a moment's confusion I realise they are the wings of moths, along with a few butterflies – mostly large yellow underwings and small tortoiseshells – lying restful in death.

The neat arrangement of these remnants of once-living insects suggests that they have been placed here deliberately, like some sort of votive offering. But I suspect they have simply been dropped by bats, roosting somewhere in the rafters above my head. I recall watching a bat chasing moths in the neighbouring farmyard on a warm, July night; this must be where he brought them, before dismembering and eating their tiny but nutritious bodies.

In the fields, throughout the shortening hours of daylight, scattered flocks of starlings gather to feed. Some follow herds of cattle, and as the beasts wander slowly across the muddy surface of the field, the birds nip in behind them to grab worms and insects exposed by their heavy hooves. Occasionally the starlings rise up into the air and wheel around; so that by late afternoon, as the sun begins to set, their flickering wings glow orange in the fading light.

At night, the mist returns, gentle wisps hanging above the rhynes; then, as the temperature drops, spreading out over the lanes and fields.

❀

LATE NOVEMBER IS a very quiet time in nature's calendar; not just in this parish, but across much of Britain. The only sounds I hear are the occasional chattering of sparrows as I pass one of the parish farmyards, the trilling of an optimistic wren awaiting the far-off spring, and the quiet, soft piping of a bullfinch hidden deep in a willow hedge.

Fieldfare numbers are building up now, with flocks of a hundred or more perching in the tall trees and hedgerows, feeding greedily on crimson hawthorn berries. As I approach, there is a characteristic launching, with a slightly panicked flapping of wings that never look quite strong enough to lift the heavy body into the air. Then they all rise up, as a crow sounds a high-pitched cry of alarm. A small, taut shape shoots out of the hawthorn hedgerow: a male sparrowhawk, twisting and turning in pursuit of a bird not much smaller than he is; his T-shaped silhouette shooting low across the landscape as clouds of birds panic in the skies above.

A few minutes later, the sparrowhawk has moved on, and the fieldfares have settled back in the topmost twigs of the hawthorns. A constant, soft, chattering sound fills the air, as if they are discussing the event I have just witnessed. Fanciful, I know, but this murmur of sound is clearly a response to the passing of the predator.

The more time I spend in the parish, the more I become sensitive to these subtle changes in sight and sound. This is a skill all naturalists pick up over the years, but it is heightened on my journey through time and seasons in the same, small, enclosed place. It goes much deeper than mere knowledge; and almost feels as if I am becoming part of the landscape and its wildlife. I find it comforting to know that as I get older, and my physical horizons inevitably begin to diminish, I shall never get bored with what I see, hear and find in this country parish.

❀

IT'S NOT YET December, but from time to time, in place of the usual damp, dull grey Novembers, we get an early fall of snow or, as the locals call it, 'cold fallings'. It always comes as a surprise to some: last night one driver misjudged the corner at the end of our lane, and paid the inevitable price. His car is now lying on its side in the rhyne, awaiting rescue.

On the last Saturday of the month, the day of the church Christmas bazaar, temperatures hover around zero. The rhynes are half frozen, in that mushy state between water and ice, but still attract flocks of starlings, which gather precariously at the foot of the steep banks to take little sips of water. The high points of the Mendips and Poldens, along with Brent Knoll, are covered with a fine layer of white powder. There is just enough snow for the village children to go sledging; or there would be, if their parents didn't have better things to do, such as the Christmas shopping.

What remains of the parish birdlife is stung into urgent action, as the combination of hard weather and fewer hours of daylight means that it is much harder to find food. Jackdaws, rooks and the odd crow take to the air in loose flocks; tits and finches congregate on garden bird-feeders; and along the back lanes of the parish, a new influx of thousands – perhaps tens of thousands – of winter thrushes has arrived.

Redwings and fieldfares are simply everywhere. They rise from the tops of the hedgerows, flitting along fifty or a hundred yards, before pulling their wings close to their body and plummeting back down again. These are newly arrived birds, forced south and west by the snow; an altogether more substantial replacement for the light and airy birds of spring and summer. The swallows left us barely six weeks ago, but are now living among the big game of the African savannah, with the sun warming their backs. Here, we continue to shiver in the cold.

DECEMBER

I T I S T H E coldest, frostiest morning of this unexpected early-winter cold snap. In the weak warmth of the sun's first rays, the world has turned not white, but shades of buff, brown and yellow. The tall stands of reeds, the hard earth in the fields, even the hedgerows – now trimmed as close as a military haircut – all bask in the glow of this early-morning light.

The birds fit this colour scheme too. Reed buntings sit on the broad, flat tops of the hedges, their plumage fluffed up against the cold, while wrens and song thrushes flit in and out of the thick foliage beneath. How changed is the song thrush from the loud, confident songster of earlier in the year. Now he is furtive and solitary, in sharp contrast to his gregarious cousins the redwings and fieldfares.

The fields, long since cut for silage, are now a mixture of short grass and thick, loamy mud. In the bare twigs of the ash trees blue tits and great tits chatter, and the odd robin and wren call to one another. Occasionally, when the mood takes them, they utter a brief burst of song; the sweet notes piercing the winter air with the distant promise of spring. From time to time a new sound appears: a frantic, high-pitched seep-seep-seep, accompanied by a rather soft, chirping note. A dozen long-tailed tits flit along the hedgerow, separate yet together, as if connected to one another by invisible strands of elastic.

When you are close to a flock of long-tailed tits, the sense of intimacy is palpable. It's not quite that they don't notice us, more as if they don't really care. By now the juveniles have moulted their first soft, coffee-and-cream-coloured plumage, and are indistinguishable from their parents. But they still stick together; as a friend of mine sagely noted, this is the only small bird that spends Christmas with its family.

Like most birds, the long-tailed tits don't seem bothered by the light shower drifting down from a charcoal-grey sky – 'leppery weather' in the local parlance. Unless the rain gets heavier they won't bother to seek shelter, but will keep searching for food, the soft raindrops bouncing off their delicate feathers.

Following a couple of cold spells back in the 1980s, a run of mild winters has led to a boom in numbers of this charismatic bird. The recent switch back to hard winters, with snow and below-freezing temperatures, has hit them less hard than we might have imagined; perhaps because they have learned, in the interim, to visit feeders in our gardens. Although they rarely stand up to their larger, tougher relatives, their ability to nip in and grab a few life-giving seeds has enabled them to survive even the coldest spells.

❀

THE NEXT MORNING Jack Frost has returned with a vengeance, and now the scenery really has turned whiter-than-white: white trees, white hedgerows, white grass, white roofs and white sky. This is landscape in crystal form, only punctuated by the staccato notes of black birds as they dash across the sky or gather in the fields: chords of starlings, followed by the occasional crow, jackdaw or rook. And one brief splash of colour: a flock of goldfinches, whose crimsons and golds illuminate the landscape like a coloured frame added to an old black-and-white film.

Later, as the sun sets over Brent Knoll, a low ridge of cloud hangs over the Mendips, while a darker, more menacing wave arrives from the west. A strong, full moon begins to rise, gradually illuminating the flat, white landscape. A lone buzzard perches on top of a hawthorn hedge, surveying his misty white kingdom. Apart from a distant dog barking, and the hum of the milking parlour at Perry Farm, all is quiet; when it is as cold as this, no bird will waste energy in song. In the rhyne by the farm a lone heron stands rigid on the ice, as if fixed permanently to the spot. On catching sight of me he has just enough energy to flap those huge, rounded wings and fly away. I hope he finds some water, somewhere in this frozen land.

Soft, ghost-like, the mist surges westwards from the darkness, creating a blanket of vapour over the layer of snow beneath, like a counterpane laid carefully over a duvet. As it finally covers the land, the tops of trees and hedgerows poke out as if grasping towards the last few minutes of daylight, before they too are swathed in the mist.

❀

AFTER A BRIEF thaw, comes another big freeze. A week before Christmas a cold front arrives overnight, and dumps a good 6 inches of snow on every available skyward-facing surface. Trees, power lines, roofs, chimneys, goalposts, bushes, reeds, hedgerows and the rock-hard earth are all completely covered with this increasingly familiar white substance. With the coming of the snow, the yews and gravestones in the churchyard are trimmed with white, making this timeless scene even more beautiful than usual. A mistle thrush chatters as he defends the scarlet yew berries against all comers, while beneath his perch discarded ones lie like drops of blood in the snow.

Inside the church, there is, rather appropriately, a white wedding. As the bride and groom emerge into the sunlight on their new life together, they are accompanied by a joyful chorus of bells from the church tower. There is something familiar, yet strangely odd, about this classic scene. Familiar, because when we were growing up snow was a regular occurrence, even here in the milder south-west of the country. Odd, because over the past few decades we have grown to assume that snow, along with short trousers, playing kiss-chase and collecting stamps, was something we had left behind with the passing of childhood. So to see it in such all-encompassing glory, taking over the land like an invading army, brings a strange clash between nostalgia and reality.

Meanwhile, amid this unreal scene, we all face the reality of the inconvenience the white stuff has brought along with it. We are unable to complete our Christmas shopping, travel to friends or relatives, or even drive to the supermarket; so Tom and Anne at the village stores are doing a roaring trade in essential supplies. We are all confined to barracks for the duration, making last-minute mince pies, wrapping presents, or simply slumped in front of the television, enjoying its festive offerings.

❁

IT IS AN hour or so before dusk, on Christmas Eve, and the landscape has turned completely monochrome. Far away to the north-east, at King's College Chapel in Cambridge, a lone chorister is singing the opening notes of 'Once in Royal David's City', a moment that for me always marks the true beginning of Christmas. Feeling the need to escape the warm fug of central heating, and get some cold, fresh air back into my lungs, I take a late-afternoon walk, accompanied by my youngest son George, my brother-in-law Luke, and his two very energetic dogs.

Apart from the dogs' frenzied activity, the world is almost lifeless: with no sound, and hardly any movement. Yet wildlife always retains the capacity to surprise, and as we trudge across Blackford Moor, a large, heavy-looking bird flies out of the hedge right next to us. It is a short-eared owl, one of the few members of its family to hunt by day. The owl flaps low across the field, its browns, blacks and greys standing out vividly against the white;

perches briefly on top of a broad hedge, and turns to stare back at me with its piercing yellow eyes. It then flies high towards the east, briefly hassled by a passing crow; its deep, powerful wingbeats reminding me of a huge, slow-motion moth.

Short-eared owls were once a regular winter sight, not just here in Somerset, but across much of Britain. In recent years they have declined, and nowadays any sighting, especially one as close and intimate as this, is a special event. An unexpected and delightful present, just before the sun sets on Christmas Eve.

As we wander home, I reflect on the dramatic shift in our expectations of the nature of winter. Only a few years ago, I remember thinking that my youngest children would probably never have the thrill of making a snowman, or enjoying a snowball fight. Now they simply assume that with the coming of winter, there will be snow. And although the lack of falling snow means this does not technically count as a white Christmas, try telling that to the village children, as they play gleefully in the thick white stuff on Christmas morning.

❀

WE HAVE REACHED that strange no-man's-land between Christmas and New Year; what a friend of mine calls the 'Winterval'. Turkeys, mince pies and Christmas puddings have been consumed; presents opened, played with and discarded; relatives welcomed, fed and dispatched. A few miles up the M5, at the Cribbs Causeway shopping mall, the 'January sales' are in full swing, even though New Year is still several days away. Thankfully, the natural world provides an alternative, and rather more satisfying, experience.

A couple of miles beyond the River Brue, the southern boundary of the parish, another winter dawn breaks over Catcott Lows. As the mist rises from the cold ground, revealing the silhouette of Glastonbury Tor, I begin to lose any sense of feeling in my fingertips. All around me, a shrill chorus of whistles pierces the chill air. It is the unmistakable sound of hundreds of wigeon, the most striking and handsome of all our dabbling ducks.

Today, a thousand or so wigeon, together with smaller flocks of teal, mallard and shoveler, are crammed in and around a small hole in the ice. Looking more closely at the plumage of a male wigeon, I am reminded that so many colours and patterns in the natural world defy my powers of description.

From a distance, the overall impression is of a grey body framed with black and white, and a brown head. But when I take a closer look, I can see that the 'grey' is made up of a series of narrow, wavy black lines on a white background. Duck aficionados call these vermiculations, from the Latin for worm, as they are supposed to resemble the wavy pattern of a worm's trail. Close up, the 'brown' head is a deep, rich chestnut, set off with a broad stripe of yellow-ochre, as if someone has casually run a paintbrush down the front of the bird's face. And what colour is that breast – pink? Not quite, but not quite orange, either.

The wigeon's shape is pleasing, too: with its pointed tail, high forehead, and short, grey bill tipped with black, ideal for grazing. For unlike most other ducks, the wigeon finds most of its food not in the water, but by walking slowly and deliberately across the wet meadows, using its bill like a pair of nail-scissors to cut the tips off the short, sweet grass.

Of all the birds here before me, the wigeon have travelled the furthest. Although a few hundred pairs breed in northern Britain, their numbers are massively swelled each autumn, when close to half a million birds arrive here from their breeding grounds in Iceland, Scandinavia and northern Russia. Because these areas freeze up during the winter, the wigeon must travel southwards and westwards, seeking out the more benevolent, maritime climate of Britain and Ireland.

Here on the Somerset Levels we have our fair share of these engaging ducks, but another winter visitor from Siberia, Bewick's swan, has all but disappeared. Named after the nineteenth-century engraver, publisher and political radical Thomas Bewick, small flocks of these wild swans have always spent the winter here, filling the air with their yelping cries. But in the past decade numbers have fallen away, and nowadays only a handful overwinter on the levels. Most are well to the south, in the vast waterlogged fields around the villages of Muchelney, Stoke St Gregory and Curry Rivel, whose very names reflect the long and fascinating history of this unique landscape.

Even without the Bewick's swans, though, the sight and sound of more than a thousand dabbling ducks lifts the spirits. My encounter with them reinforces the continuity of this place and its wildlife over time, much in the same way as the distant backdrop of Glastonbury Tor reminds me of our human presence here across the centuries.

❀

A DARK SILHOUETTE materialises out of the grey sky; its sheer power marking it out as something different from the crowd. It is a peregrine: the fastest living creature on the planet. Ever alert, the ducks take off, rising as one organism from the ice. Each individual bird sticks as close as possible to its nearest neighbour, trying desperately to avoid being singled out by this mighty predator. At first, this looks like an unequal contest: surely the hunter's speed, power and strength will triumph? But the battle between predator and prey is far more equal than it looks: each has co-evolved in a constant 'arms race' to outwit the other, and more often than not the hunt ends in failure for the hunter.

The peregrine – a big female – has a very short timespan to make a crucial decision: which individual duck will she go for? She singles out a straggling wigeon on the edge of the flock, and zeroes in with her piercing dark eyes, up to ten times sharper than my own. As she approaches, the ducks perform their own evasion strategy: twisting and turning to confuse their attacker. Each time the peregrine swoops low over the surface of the water she must take great care: unlike the wigeon, she does not have an oil gland with which to waterproof her plumage. Should she inadvertently land on the water, she may become water-logged and drown.

Time is on the ducks' side, too. For like a cheetah pursuing a gazelle, the peregrine is a sprinter, able to channel her energy into a sudden burst of speed in order to make the fatal blow. But as each second passes without a kill, the muscles in her wings begin to tire, and the chances of the wigeon escaping increase. Eventually, with a rapid twist of a wing, she makes a sudden change in direction, heading upwards into the sky. She has given up, and the wigeon sense it, their whistles becoming gradually less agitated as they float gently down to earth.

Minutes later, and it is as if the drama never happened. The wigeon are back on the ground, waddling across the frosted grass and getting down to the business of the day: feeding. The peregrine is long gone, in search of other targets to chase. But as I lift my binoculars, I realise my heart is beating much faster than usual.

❀

DECEMBER HAS BEEN, according to the Met Office, the coldest since records began a century ago. Following three hard winters in a row, this return to a traditional pattern of seasons – cold winters, late springs and warm summers – appears to have been a tonic for Britain's wildlife. Nature, so the theory goes, works best when our weather patterns revert to normal. So hibernating creatures stay put instead of waking too early; birds nest at the right time; flowers bloom, insects buzz and migrants arrive when they should; and all is right with the world.

It would be easy to assume that this suggests that the planet has somehow pressed the reset button, and that from now on we shall experience more typical weather patterns. But I'm not so sure. Even as we have shivered in the snow, much of the rest of the world has been experiencing far higher temperatures than usual. Taken as a whole, all the evidence points to the conclusion that the earth is undergoing its most rapid period of warming since the end of the last Ice Age. Ironically, even the recent heavy snowfalls are an indicator of this: extreme weather events, including droughts, storms, floods, and freezes, are all signs of an unstable and rapidly warming climate.

As are the changes we are already seeing in our fauna and flora, especially here in the south of Britain; changes I have witnessed during my own lifetime. When I first became interested in birds there were just two different kinds of heron breeding in Britain: the common and widespread grey heron, and the much rarer bittern. Today, there are up to half a dozen species living within a cycle ride of my home, including those we used to see only on holidays to the Mediterranean.

Once, any white object in the fields of the parish was either a swan, or a plastic tub containing food for sheep. Today it is just as likely to be a little egret, whose elegant posture and Persil-white plumage have become a regular sight. One winter no fewer than four egrets took up residence in the rhyne at the back of our house, each standing poised and still before striking out like a hunter with a spear, to grab a passing fish with that sharp, pointed bill.

Taking the children to school one day, I saw a lone egret flying overhead. Something about its slow, deliberate wingbeats made me realise that this was the little egret's much larger relative, the great white egret. Not so very long ago this huge white bird – the height of a grey heron, with a wingspan of almost 6 feet – was an extreme rarity in Britain. But in the past few years it has become a permanent resident here on the Somerset Levels. With as many as half a dozen birds living here, it will surely breed in the next year or two.

Another species of small, white heron already has. A few years ago, on a fine sunny day in May, I was driving across Tealham Moor with the children when we spotted three egrets feeding among the grazing cows. Something about their small size and hunched shape struck me as different; sure enough, they were cattle egrets. That very same year they bred in a heronry close by; the first ever breeding record for Britain.

At first sight this seemed extraordinary, for this is the bird we usually see perched on the backs of elephants and buffaloes in nature films about the African savannah. But this wasn't a chance occurrence, for of all the birds in the world, the cattle egret is among the most skilled at adapting. Originally native to the warmer regions of Europe, Asia and Africa, it has, during the past century or so, managed to colonise South America, North America and Australasia. Now the species is surging northwards through Europe, and in the next few years is likely to become a permanent member of Britain's birdlife.

Birds aren't the only creatures taking advantage of global warming: insects such as moths and dragonflies are also able to move northwards as the climate heats up. Here in Somerset we are well placed to receive the expected influx of continental European species, such as that hummingbird hawkmoth I saw on my buddleia bush back in July. And during the next few decades, if the warming trend continues, I confidently expect exotic, colourful birds such as the hoopoe and bee-eater to breed regularly here in southern Britain.

But there's a downside to global warming, too. In the longer term, we know that any rise in temperatures is likely to have catastrophic consequences. Extreme weather events, and a change in the timing of the seasons, will seriously affect the wildlife of this parish, and indeed the whole of Britain, in unpredictable ways. We may assume that adaptable species such as crows and magpies, dandelions and daisies, cabbage whites and foxes, will all thrive. Predators and scavengers are also likely to do well. But any plant or animal that requires a specialised habitat, and those that migrate, will almost certainly struggle to survive in the longer term.

For me, one of the greatest pleasures of living in the English countryside is the way we ourselves become part of the natural cycle of the seasons. We celebrate the coming of the swallows in spring, and witness their departure in autumn; our hearts leap when we see the first snowdrops; and we look out for the budding of the trees followed, a few months later, by the falling of their leaves. All these experiences bind us tightly together with the living world. In the case of a global migrant like the swallow, they also connect us with people we shall never see and never know; people who live thousands of miles away from this little country village.

But if the pattern of the seasons is broken – if what we are seeing now is not a return to the status quo but a final, valedictory farewell – then the connections between us and the natural world may also be shattered, perhaps for ever. If swallows fail to adapt, then we will not simply have lost a wild creature, but also everything that crea-ture means to us. For some icons of the natural world, this has already happened. As I noted earlier, across much of

Britain, the cuckoo has now become a mere folk memory, its sound dying away as the years go by.

❁

As New Year's Eve dawns, the natural world has come full circle, and we are back where we began. Yet even in the depths of winter there are signs of life, if you know where to look for them.

In the corner of an old wooden railway carriage in my back garden, a small tortoiseshell butterfly is hiding among the spiders' webs, wings closed to conceal its bright colours. It will stay here all winter, before emerging again on the first warm day of the year, to suck nectar from the early-spring flowers.

Underneath the railway carriage, the toad that wandered into our home a few months ago is also hibernating; just like the slow-worm in the compost heap, the bats in the rafters of the barn, and any hedgehogs that managed to survive the annual burning of the log-piles on the Fifth of November.

Small mammals such as voles, mice and shrews stay active, though well out of sight. Snow is no problem for them, as they make burrows beneath its soft white layer, and continue to search for morsels of food.

But the predators that hunt these little creatures – the barn owls and kestrels – are having a lean time of it. The resident kestrel by Lower Splott Farm can still be seen perched on his telegraph pole or, occasionally, hovering in search of food; but the barn owls along the lane to Chapel Allerton, those at the top of Kingsway, and the pair south of the River Brue, have all disappeared.

Waterbirds are having a tough time, too. The village moorhens still potter about in the rhynes; herons stand statuesque on the ice; and a snipe, just arrived from the north, probes his bill into the half-frozen mud. Further downstream, a kingfisher sits, a beacon of blue and orange against the white, patiently waiting for a fish to appear.

The fields of the parish are quiet. The occasional buzzard and lapwing accompany small flocks of rooks and jackdaws, while the high-pitched trill of a wren pierces the heavy silence. By night, hares, roe deer and badgers roam these same fields. When morning comes, the only evidence of their nocturnal wanderings is a few prints in the snow.

Soon after the break of dawn, vast squadrons of star-lings fly low towards the north-west, on the way from their night-time roost to feed on the mudflats of Bridgwater Bay. As dusk falls, they make the return journey, the soft whoosh of their wings reaching my ears a fraction of a second before they appear overhead. Seconds later, they are gone.

Everywhere I look, colour has drained from the land-scape, and the pinks, purples, yellows and greens of earlier in the year are but a distant memory. I struggle to recall the spring chorus of birdsong, the gentle summer buzzing of bumblebees, and the last, autumnal flicker of butterflies' wings.

I find it hard to believe that many of the birds that hatched out just a few months ago in the barns, among the reedbeds and deep inside the hedgerows of the village are now half a world away, under African skies. But soon they will respond to an unseen signal, and begin their long and arduous journey north.

And one fine day next spring, as I wander along the back lanes of this quiet country parish, I shall see and hear them once again, bringing joy and gladness to my heart.

Acknowledgements

THE GENESIS OF a book like this is essentially personal, but its progress from idea to finished work involves many people. My agent Broo Doherty was, as always, wonderfully encouraging and perceptive, and helped me to decide that this was indeed the right time to write about the wildlife of my home patch. At Square Peg, Rosemary Davidson commissioned the book and guided it to its conclusion with her usual enthusiasm and skill, while Simon Rhodes and Iree Pugh oversaw the design. I would particularly like to thank Chris Wormell, the cover artist, and Harry Brockway, whose splendid scraperboard illustrations truly evoke the passing of the seasons and the comings and goings of the parish wildlife. At Random House, I should also like to thank Kate Bland, Ruth Warburton, Alison Faulkner, Will Smith and Vicki Watson, for all their efforts to promote the book.

Several people either accompanied me on my walks and cycle rides around the parish, or gave me the benefit of their experience and observations. In no particular order they are: Peter Marren, Adrian Boots, Alison Tutt (and her children Lewis and Harriet), David Ballance, Ed Drewitt, Ruth Peacey, Luke Davie and Graham Coster.

In and around the village itself, I especially want to thank my neighbours: Mick Lockyer, Rick and Heather

Popham and their family, Marc and Dawn Talbot, Steve Short, John Creber and his grandson James, Val Stone, Dennis Kurle, Susie and Kevin Fowler, Tom and Anne Hanlon, Mike ('the jolly butcher'), Jon Glauert and the children and staff at Avalon Camps, the organisers of Mark Harvest Home, and all the villagers of Mark and the surrounding parishes, whose love of their local wildlife is passionate and profound.

My dear friend Sue Caola kindly read the manuscript and made many helpful suggestions, especially on the history of the village and the surrounding areas. I also owe a great debt to Pamela Slocombe, whose book *Mark: a Somerset Moorland Village*, was a valuable source of historical information. I continue to be inspired by two great writers, Gilbert White and John Clare, both of whom understood the significance of the local, and what it can tell us about the bigger picture.

My wife Suzanne, and my children, David, James, Charlie, George and Daisy, are a constant inspiration. The younger children, in particular, show a passion for wildlife which I hope they will retain as they grow up in these wonderful rural surroundings. We moved here from London five years ago for a better quality of life, and this book is in part a celebration of our leap of faith. It was, without doubt, the best thing we ever did.

I owe a special debt of thanks to my friend and colleague, the broadcaster and radio producer Brett Westwood. Brett accompanied me on a memorable cycle ride around the parish on a glorious day at midsummer. He is the finest naturalist I know, and as we made our way along the back lanes and droves he opened my eyes to a whole new world of wild flowers and insects.

Finally, I would like to pay tribute to the wonderful wildlife of this parish; not least the two species which give this book its title, the wild hares and hummingbirds.

www.vintage-books.co.uk